Collision Blast Basic Auto Body and Paint Training

Where The Experts Are The Authors

CollisionBlast.com

E-Book Training Course

Basic Auto Body and Paint Training

Knowledge and Writing

Excellence

Donnie Smith

iPage

ISBN:1460914929
ISBN-13: 9781460914922

ii P a g e

DEDICATION

This book is dedicated to the people who have read my articles and watched my training videos and encouraged me to provide additional training.

Thanks for the inspiration and support.

CONTENTS

Basic Auto Body Repair Training Modules

Resources Bonus Material

WELCOME

Hi, Donnie Smith here and I would like to thank for purchasing my auto body and paint training book. In this book, I am going to give you some techniques and tips of how to repair and paint your car.

This book also includes a web enhanced website, which has all of the content in the book, plus updates, Q&A section and much more bonus information. To gain access to the members-only website visit www.TeachMeHow.info and click on the Members link. You will be asked to provide a username and password. The **username is: simple** and the **password is: training**

I hope that you enjoy and find value in this book. Any feedback, good or bad, would be very helpful to me.

Thanks,

Donnie Smith

Donnie Smith

Your Virtual How-To Basic Auto Body and Paint Book Training Course

ABOUT THE BOOK

By reading this book you will learn from years of experience, but more importantly, you will eliminate many of the common mistakes that I have seen students make, and mistakes that I have made along the way. I have also produced and included many of my free training videos and I have searched the internet for additional relevant videos and other resources that I believe will help you learn how to repair and paint your car or reach whatever your training goal is.

You will also gain access to my web enhanced course that will help you excel through the training process.

MODULE 1 SAFETY

"Are you Worth 1 Million Dollars?"

You know it, I had to mention safety before we kick off. You always hear "safety first" at safety meetings, but many technicians think safety is a lot of hype and ignore the safety policies. So is safety really that important?

Let's Talk Cars

First, since we're all about cars, not safety, let's talk about restoring an awesome car. Let's say we have an unlimited budget to build a million dollar ride. You know, a car like Chip Foose at Foose Design would build. Of course, it would take hours and hours of labor and thousands of dollars to get it there, but the end result would be well worth the wait and money. Could you imagine having a ride worth one million dollars? I'm sure that you would take a lot of pride in it. I know that I would. Would you take care of it? What about storage, would you keep it in the garage or put it out back in the weather? I'm sure that you would do everything that you could to protect the car from being damaged.

Another Question

If someone offered you a million dollar car like this, would you exchange it for your eyesight? What about a leg, or would you trade your life for it? I am assuming you answered no, as these things are priceless to us. I would not want to even exchange my eyesight or life for a billion dollars. While most of you would agree, we are quick to ignore safety and grab a grinder and start grinding, weld without a welding helmet, paint without a paint respirator, or many other things that could affect our health without thinking twice about it. If you're willing to take good care of a car, don't you think you should take care of yourself?

Over-Exaggerating

Well, this is over-exaggerated. Or is it? There are many eye injuries and painters who have to leave the collision repair industry every year due to becoming sensitive to paint chemicals. It really happens, but the good news is that most injuries are preventable.

How To Prevent Injuries

It would take a while to explain all of the PPE (Personal Protective Equipment) that needs to be used, but I will highlight a few of them.

1. **Eye Protection** – Most schools require eye protection to be worn at all times in the shop area, but I see a lot of body shops that do not require eye protection. However, I would highly recommend that you get in the habit of wearing eye protection. Eyesight is too valuable to lose.

2. **Dust masks** – When sanding or grinding wear an approved dust mask. This will prevent you from breathing all of the products being sanded and other debris that is not healthy for you.

3. **Respirator** – The catalyzed clears and primers that are out there should not be taken lightly. They have chemicals that will mess you up. Wear an approved respirator when spraying any coatings.

4. **Gloves** – Chemical resistant gloves should be worn when working with chemicals. This will prevent the chemicals from entering your body through your skin.

5. **Hearing Protection** – You may not need to wear hearing protection at all times, but if there is grinding, air chiseling, or other loud things going on, protect your hearing.

There are many other PPE and safety procedures to consider before working in a shop area. I hope when you answer the question of who is saying safety first, you think of yourself. Forget about the policies and procedures, keep yourself safe....... as we just discussed, you're worth a million dollars.

I know that safety is not one of the most interesting subjects, but it is one of the most important. If you get hurt, you may not be able to perform this type of work for fun or for a career. Therefore, I have included several safety training resources. I am using CareerSafe to provide the training for this topic, as that is what they do. I'll leave the safety to them and I will concentrate on what I do....auto body and paint training.

Module 1 Resources

Visit www.TeachMeHow.info and sign into the members website to access the resources below.

Audio
1. •Module 1 Text Podcast

Videos
1. •DuPont 6H Video

PowerPoints
1. •Introduction to OSHA PowerPoint
2. •Bloodborne Pathogens PowerPoint
3. •Electrical Safety PowerPoint
4. •Emergency Action Plans PowerPoint
5. •Ergonomics PowerPoint
6. •HazCom PowerPoint
7. •Machine Guarding PowerPoint
8. •Material Handling PowerPoint
9. •Personal Protective Equipment (PPE) PowerPoint

Product Information
1. •3M Paint Respirator
2. •Black Nitrile Gloves
3. •Dust Masks

4. •<u>Ear Plugs</u>

5. •<u>Safety Glasses</u>

Product Technical Sheet

1. •No product technical sheets for this module

MSDS

1. •No product MSDS for this module

Websites

1. •<u>www.CaeerSafe.com</u>
2. •<u>www.osha.com</u>
3. •<u>www.sp2.org</u>
4. •<u>Virtual Collision/Paint Shop</u>

Module 1 Training Activity

Read or listen to module 1 text. Next click on the 9 PowerPoints and read each slide. I have also included three websites for you to view. There is additional training (free and paid) on each website for you to consider. Question: **Think of a time that a safety procedure or equipment protected you from injury; or a time that you were injured due to insufficient equipments or lack of policies in place. Post in the Q&A section.** Lastly, Complete Module 1 Quiz.

Step-By-Step

Not a lot of step-by-step for this module. The most important advice that I can offer is to read all product, tool, and equipment labels and manuals before using or operating.

Additional Resources

I have many additional resources that will be included at the end of this book. However, I do not want to include them under each module. As an instructor, I am aware that too much is not always a good thing. Information overload may leave you feeling behind, confused, and/or burned-out. Therefore, concentrate on the information and resources in each module. Once you have completed the book, you can explore the additional resources. Again, don't stress about getting through all of the additional resources all at once. Remember simplicity...keep it simple.

Module 1 Safety Quiz

Once you have completed the module content, take the module 1 quiz below. Please note that you must score 75% or higher to receive a certificate. This is a short quiz with only 10 questions. There is not a time limit set on this quiz so take your time. Find the correct answer if you do not know for sure. **The objective of this quiz is to help you learn the information if you do not know the answer, not guessing**. Good luck!

MODULE 2 VEHICLE HISTORY

"They don't make them like they used to."

The First Cars

1. •The first motor cars were nothing more than a buggy and engine. (Generally repaired by blacksmiths and carpenters. These cars were very expensive, which only the wealthy could afford)

2. •Model T was the first car mass production on an assembly line in 1908. (Ford's vision was to produce an affordable car the average person could purchase)

3. •Model T's came in black only to keep the costs down. (The price came down once the assembly line was streamlined, but in 1908, the cost for a Model T started at $825. By 1913 the cost of the car was reduced to $550)

Cars in the 1960s

Cars were made the same basic way up through the 60s.

1. •Body Over Frame

2. •Rear Wheel Drive (Same concept, but the cars were very big, bulky, and heavy)

Except people in the 60s wanted SPEED! They achieved this with Big Block Motors, which created a lot of horsepower. (The Birth of Hotrods, Rat Fink, Flames, and Pin Striping.)

Cars in the 1970s
•The government placed strict fuel economy and emissions control laws.
•Customers demanded cars with increased fuel economy.
•New laws and customer demands started the automotive explosion of engineering ideas and changes in the automotive industry.

Changes to Comply with Demands and Laws
•Smaller bodied cars and smaller engines
•Aerodynamics (Increase Fuel Mileage)
•Lighter cars by using different materials and designs
•More work-hardened areas created during formation of panel (Body Lines)
•Safety

Construction of Interstate Highways + Higher Speed Limits + More High Performance Cars = Accidents and More Deaths from Auto Accidents

Federal Laws were passed to regulate safety. These laws included:
•Installation of seatbelts
•Safety glass windshields
•Head restraints
•In 1979, the first driver side airbag was introduced

•Airbags are mandatory in motor cars produced after 1990
•Unibody Torque Boxes: Allow controlled twisting and crushing
•Crush Zones: Made to collapse during collision (To act as an absorber, absorbing the impact)

Modern Day Cars
•Carbon Fiber Parts
•Aluminum Parts
•More Plastic Parts
•High Strength Steel
•Boron Steel
•Unibody Construction
•Space Frame Construction
•Computer
•Hybrid Cars

Now they even have cars that will tell you when you're lost, where to turn, and parallel park for you.

Conclusion
While the modern day cars appear to be made cheap and unsafe, they are actually designed to crush or collapse, while transferring the energy around the stronger passenger compartment to protect the passengers from injury.

There is considerably more damage to modern day cars during a collision than the older vehicles, which gives the perception that "they don't make them like they used to." However, in reality the cars are taking the impact instead of the passengers.

The lesson was designed to give you a little history, but to also emphasize that just a hammer, dolly, and a few wrenches are not going to repair today's cars.

I didn't want to get to carried away with the history, but it is good to have a basic idea of how we got to where we are today. Henry Ford was an amazing man and absolutely changed the automotive world. It amazes me to see how far we have advanced in the past 100 years.

Module 2 Resources

Visit www.TeachMeHow.info and sign into the members website to access the resources below.

Audios
1. •Module 2 Text Podcast
Videos
1. •The Model T - 100 Years Later
2. •Automobile History
3. •Modern Day Vehicles

PowerPoints
1. •No PowerPoints for this module

Product Information
1. •No product information for this module

Product Technical Sheet
1. •No product technical sheets for this module

Websites
1. •History of the Automobile

Module 2 Training Activity
Read the vehicle overview article and/or listen to module 2 podcast, watch the two videos, and visit

the history of automobiles website.   Question: **What do you think has been the most significant change in the auto industry in the past 30 years? Post in the Q&A Discussion.** Lastly, complete module 2 quiz.

Step-By-Step

1.   •No step-by-step procedures for this module

Additional Resources

I have many additional resources that will be included at the end of this book. However, I do not want to include them under each module. As an instructor, I am aware that too much is not always a good thing. Information overload may leave you feeling behind, confused, and/or burned-out. Therefore, concentrate on the information and resources in each module. Once you have completed the book, you can explore the additional resources. Again, don't stress about getting through all of the additional resources all at once. Remember simplicity...keep it simple.

Module 2 History Quiz

Once you have completed the module content, take the module 2 quiz below. Please note that you must score 75% or higher to receive a certificate. This is a short quiz with only 10 questions. There is not a time limit set on this quiz so take your time. Find the correct answer if you do not know for sure. **The objective of this quiz is to help you learn the information if you do not know the answer, not guessing**. **Good luck!**

MODULE 3 METAL STRAIGHTENING
"First In, Last Out"

We've touched on safety and the history of automobiles, now let's start talking repairs. In this module we are going to cover metal straightening. There are different types of steel, such as mild steel, high strength steel, ultra high strength steel, boron, etc. However, this module is going to focus on mild steel, as mild steel is used on many of the body parts. If you restore older cars, probably all of the steel that you work with will be mild steel. Many of the other types of steels are used on structural parts.

First we're going to talk about the difference between older and newer cars and the repair considerations that you will need to make before repairing.

The Difference Between Repairing Early Model Cars and Cars of Today - Metal Straightening

Repairing Early Model Cars

On early model vehicles the metal was thick, which had advantages and disadvantages. First, they had a lot of metal to work with. This allowed body men to hammer, dolly, and pick on the metal, then file the top surface, knocking the high areas down. Then they could repeat the process, working the metal and filing the surface level. This allowed the body man to metal finish much of the damages without the need of body fillers. This is called metal finishing. If there were still a few imperfections remaining, the body man would use lead to fill the lows and file the surface level and smooth.

Advantages and Disadvantages

The advantage they had was the possibility to straighten and work the metal without the use of fillers. If we tried to use those methods on vehicles today, we would have a hole in the part from filing through the part. If we didn't file a hole through the part, it would be very thin and weak. Another advantage of working on early model vehicles is being able to get to both sides of the panel. Vehicles today have limited access. It is hard to get behind most panels to use the hammer and dolly method. The disadvantage of working metal on early model cars was the strength of the thick steel; it was hard to move, unlock, and reshape. It took a lot more force to move the thick metal when straightening. The lead filler that was used also took more time and skill to fill the small imperfections. We are also more educated about lead today and the safety hazards of it.

Repairing Vehicles of Today

Today's vehicles are thinner and have very limited access. However, improved fillers, such as body filler, and tools have made the job easier. The most common tool to use for repairing dents is a stud nail gun. The cost of a stud nail gun ranges between $200 to $500. This tool tacks a small nail to the surface. Then you get a slide hammer or t-handle to pull on the stud nail. Therefore, you tack the nails to the low areas and lightly tap on the high areas with a body hammer. It is important to do this at the same time. Just pulling out on the low area will cause the metal to be over-pulled and stretch the metal. Just hammering in on the highs may cause the entire area to be hammered in too much. This is referred to as chasing your damage around. It is always better to have multiple forces at one time. You need to think of it as rolling the damage out, rather than hammering or beating it out. The metal wants to go back to its original shape, you just need to help persuade it to. Forcing metal will result in stretched metal.

KISS Keep It Simple Silly

When you have access, a hammer and dolly can be used. This is probably going to be the fastest way to repair the damage if you have access. When performing auto body repair, think of electricity. Electricity moves wherever it is easiest for it to pass through: the path of least resistance. This is why a ground wire is used on homes. If lightning hits your house, it will follow that ground wire that is attached to a ground rod that is hammered in the ground, as that is the path of least resistance. When determining how to repair a dent, just try to think of what would be easiest. Just because you have an expensive piece of equipment does not mean that you have to use it every time. If you can reach behind the panel and pull out on the low with one hand and push down on the high with the other hand, then simply use your hand to repair the damage. It may still need a little hammer and dolly work afterwards, but I have repaired many dents with nothing but my hands. Remember today's metals are thin and it does not take much to damage a part or to repair it.

Whatever It Takes

Whether you're working on early or late model vehicles, just remember to select the tools that will make the job easiest to repair. Don't overwork the thin metal on late model vehicles, as the metals are thin. The use of body filler will help repair the surface back to its original shape.

Getting Started

We're ready to jump in and get started, but there are a few more things to do first. I know, it seems like we're never going to get started. However, remember in the beginning I mentioned that I was going to help you eliminate many of the mistakes that I made in my career. These first few steps are a few of those things. So please follow each step without rushing through and pulling damage.

Paint and Body Work Is Like Going On A Hot Date – First Things First

If you have ever been on a hot date you should be able to take the first steps to performing auto body and paint work. First, I will describe the dating process, then I'll relate it to working on cars.

Preparing For The Date

I still remember when I first started dating when I was younger. When I was in high school I did a lot of outdoor labor. Hauling pipe, working outside in lumber yards, welding cow panels, and other types of work like this. At the end of the day, you could say I was quite sweaty and dirty, but I did not seem to get tired then. I wish that I still had some of the energy that I had then! Anyway, when the work was done, I would hit the shower to get ready for the night. I would shower to remove the body sweat and odors, as I did not want my date to smell B.O. Then I would get my hair just right, yes, I had a mullet, and of course I would brush my teeth extra well. I did not want to knock my date out with my breath. I would take every necessary step to ensure that I was ready for the night.

Dating With Confidence

When I went on the date I would have the confidence that everything was ready to impress the date. If I had the chance to sit next to her, talk, or even kiss, I knew that she would not be grossed out with bad breath or sweat.

This is how I remember getting ready for a date, however, I am not saying this is how everyone prepares for a date. In fact, I know of some people who did not do much preparation before their dates. Do you think their dates went well? They could pull every smooth line and slick trick in the book, however, if the date was turned off from the start, the date is probably not going to go well and you may not have a second chance to date them.

So What Does This Have To Do With Car Paint Jobs or Body Work?

One of the common mistakes made in auto body and paint work is improper preparation. We're so excited to get started working on the car and overlook properly cleaning it. Just like being successful on a date, the first thing you need to do before beginning the work is to wash the car with dish soap and water. Then we need to wipe the car with wax and grease remover. Once this is done, you can begin repairs with confidence. However, if you skip the cleaning procedure, the repairs are going to fight you and be difficult throughout the repair process no matter how hard you try. Then the end result may have problems like lack of adhesion or fish eyes, just to name a few.

Good Advice

So here is my advice to you whether you are getting ready for a hot date or starting a collision repair or paint project. Thoroughly clean first!

Seriously, properly cleaning the vehicle is one of the most overlooked steps that have caused many problems down the road.

Dent Repair

Now that the car has been properly cleaned, the repairs can begin. Now, we can start repairing the damage. Metal can be difficult to repair, but by keeping a few ideas and strategies while straightening the repair, the metal will move back to its original shape with minimal work.

Developing A Repair Plan

Now let's discuss how to develop a repair plan. You will need to analyze how to remove a dent from an automotive part. We've determined that the panel is mild steel and repairing the damage would be a better choice than replacing the panel. Now we need to develop a repair plan and decide which repair method to use on the damage.

First In, Last Out

The first thing that you want to determine is the direction of damage. This is important so you can reverse the damage during repairs. In collision repair we have a general rule: "the first in, last out rule." This means that the direct damage or point of impact is the area first hit in an accident, which makes it the first in. Therefore, this should be the last area to repair. Direct damage is the most obvious damage as it is easy to visually see. If you try to pull the direct damage first, you will stretch the metal, pull highs in the metal, and still have lows. You are basically going to chase your damage around while work hardening the metal until the metal becomes work hardened, brittle, and cracked.

Direct and Indirect Damage

Indirect damage is the damage that is caused by the direct damage. For example, as the point of impact is pushed in, it causes the surrounding metal to slightly move as well. If pushed far enough, the indirect damage can cause misaligned body gaps, cracked seam sealer, and/or popped spot welds. The indirect damage is less noticeable as it may not be visually noticeable without close observation. The indirect damage is the damage that happened last during the accident, therefore, this damage should be repaired first. Always remember the "first in, last out" rule when developing a repair plan. This will save you hours of time and frustration when it is all done.

Choosing a Repair Method

Once the damage is analyzed, you have determined the direction of damage and the direct and indirect damage. Now it is time to decide which repair method is the best choice for the repair. If you can get to both sides of the panel a hammer and dolly method may be the easiest repair method. If you cannot gain access to both sides of the panel a stud-nail gun may be a better choice. Other considerations, such as corrosion protection and noise preventions, should be considered as well.

Don't Force The Metal, But Rather Roll The Metal Back To Its Shape.

Regardless of the repair method, the same principle applies. Start with the indirect damage and pull out on the lows and push in on the highs. You should roll the metal back into shape, rather than trying to force it back into shape. Forcing the metal back into its shape may result in highs and stretched metal. Pulling on the lows while rolling the highs out of the metal is the key to metal straightening, regardless of repair method used.

Last Bit of Advice About A Repair Plan

Plan your work and work your plan. I'm sure that you have heard of that saying, but the saying is worth gold in this industry. This applies to metal straightening, frame/unibody repair, or just about any auto repair. So keep that little tip in mind before jumping in and starting the repair.

Repair Methods

Repairing A Dent Using A Stud Nail Gun

A stud nail gun is basically a tool that welds a small stud to the metal surface. This stud provides something for the t-handle or slide hammer to grab on to. Force can then be applied to remove the damage. When using this method, you must have the repair area ground to metal as it will not work on painted surfaces. The tip must make direct contact with the metal to produce the weld. When using this method or any method, remember the rules mentioned earlier. First in, last out and roll the metal, don't just force it.

Starting at the outsides (indirect damage) weld studs to the metal. Then pull the damage as you use a body hammer to tap lightly down on the highs. Sometimes the highs may be difficult to find, but there are usually high spots. If not, I still recommend tapping lightly while pulling to relax the molecules in the metal, resulting in the metal being straightened with less force. Once the damage begins to pull out, start pulling towards the center of the damage (direct damage) using the same technique. I would also advise you to only use the slide hammer as a last resort. It is very easy to overstretch the metal using the slide hammer. I prefer using the t-handle and body hammer. Once you have completed the pull, you will need to remove the stud nails. This can be done by cutting the studs with a pair of dykesand grinding the surface smooth.

Caution: Grinding Removes Metal and Produces Heat

Keep in mind that the metal of newer cars is very thin. Therefore, you do not want to remove too much metal, making it thin and weak by over grinding. Grinding also produces heat, which is something that you want to avoid too. Keep the grinder moving around and do not hold it in one spot too long. I have actually had students shave door handles without warping the panel during the welding process. Then they get carried away with the grinder and warp the panel severely. To prevent these problems you may consider using a DA sander to remove the paint. However, a grinder will still need to be used to grind the studs smooth. Watch the stud nail gun video for more information.

Dent Removal System

There are several different types of dent removal systems, but they all use the same concept to remove damage. This system is similar to the stud nail gun, but the tip that welds to the metal surface is reused and does not require being ground off. This saves time and allows you to pull a dent out much faster. However, this type of system is much more expensive. I have also noticed through the years that students favor the stud nail gun. Perhaps they feel that this system is too big and bulky. I'm not sure, but I actually like this system better than a stud nail gun.

Other than the few differences, it is used the same way. Must be metal surface, first in, last out, and use a multiple repair method (pull on the lows and tap on the highs).

Hammer and Dolly

Hammer and dolly is probably the easiest repair method, but it requires that you have access to both side of the panel being repaired. However, newer cars have many areas that does not allow you to use hammer and dolly. There are two techniques when using hammer and dolly, hammer off dolly and hammer on dolly.

Hammer Off Dolly

Hammer off dolly is used to remove a majority of the dent. Same rules, start with the indirect damage and move towards the direct damage. Use your dolly to push your lows and your body hammer to tap down on the highs or vice-versa. Hammer off dolly should be used until the final straightening stages.

Hammer On Dolly

Hammer on dolly is used in the final stages of metal straightening to level the smaller imperfections. Please be careful not to use hammer on dolly too much, as this stretches the metal. If metal is overstretched, it must be shrunk.

Metal Shrinking

It may be necessary to shrink the metal. The metal may become stretched in the repair process or it may have been stretched during the accident causing the damage. For whatever reason, this is very easy to identify and correct. There is a term called oil canning. This is where the metal pops in and out like the top of the old style oil cans. If you are younger, you may not remember this type of oil can that I am talking about, but it is similar to a coffee can. Anyway, this is where the metal pops in and out very easy. You certainly would not want to repair a car and have someone barely lean against the car and the fender pop in. This is cause by stretched metal or too much metal in the area. They make body hammers that have small teeth (shrinking hammer) to slightly shrink the metal. However, many times it will require heat to shrink the metal. This can be performed by using a torch or stud nail gun. Heat the highest area (stretched area) to a dime size until red. Then using a body hammer lightly tap the red spot to help spread the molecules in the metal. Lastly, cool the repair with a wet sponge or compressed air. This is the only time that you want to use air or water to cool the repair area. Normally, you want to allow the areas to cool naturally.

Quenching is only used for metal shrinking.

Module 3 Resources

Visit <u>www.TeachMeHow.info</u> and sign into the members website to access the resources below.

Audio

1. •<u>Module 3 Text Podcast</u>
2. •<u>Q&A - Why Not Just Pull The Metal</u>

Videos

1. •<u>Stud Nail Gun</u>
2. •<u>Dent Removal System - Reusable Electrode</u>
3. •<u>Dent Repair 30 Minute Repair Process</u>
4. •<u>How To Hold and Dress A Body Hammer</u>
5. •<u>Body Work Hammer Technique</u>
6. •<u>Hammer on Dolly</u>
7. •<u>Heat Shrinking</u>
8. •<u>Heat Shrinking 2</u>

PowerPoints

1. •No PowerPoints for this chapter

Product Information

1. •Dish Soap - Dawn, Ivory, Etc. - Can get this at most stores.
2. •<u>Wax and Grease Remover</u>
3. •<u>3" Grinder</u>
4. •<u>3" Grinder 36 grit</u>
5. •<u>3" Grinder 50 Grit</u>
6. •<u>Stud Nail Gun</u>

7. •Dent Removal System - Trouble finding online - Check TPC
8. •Hammer and Dolly

Product Technical Sheet
1. •Wax and Grease Remover pdf

MSDS
•   Wax and Grease Remover pdf

Websites
1. •www.CollisionBlast.com
2. •Motor Guard

Module 3 Training Activity
Read module text and watch the videos. There are quite a few videos in this module and one of them is 30 minutes so you may need to set aside some time to complete this module. If you're not already a member of Collision Blast, stop by and join for free. Stop by a body shop or wrecking year to pick up a few junk fenders. If they do not have damage already make damage by using a hammer. Then try to use the methods taught in this module to repair the damage. Question: **First in, last out....why do you think it works this way? Name a few of the problems that you may have if you do not follow this rule. Add your post in the Q&A section.** Last, complete module 3 quiz.

Step-By-Step

1. •Wash the car with dish soap and water, not car soap. Many car soaps are designed to leave the wax and silicone on the finish. However, you want to strip the wax off. Like one of the Dawn slogans, "strips the grease away." That's what we want.

2. •Wipe the car with wax and grease remover.

3. •If there are any dents, repair the damage by determined repair method during the repair planning process. Remember to use the easiest repair method.

4. •If heat shrinking is needed, shrink the metal. Slight shrinking can be achieved using a cold method with a shrinking hammer. However, many time the heat method will need to be used. Use a torch or your stud nail gun with a shrinking tip, tap metal, and quench.

5. •Once the metal has been straightened, now prepare the metal for body filler. Body filler must be applied directly over steel, therefore, all coating must be removed. To do this grind or sand the surface with 36 to 50 grit sandpaper using a dual action sander or grinder. Care must be taken when using a grinder not to remove too much metal.

Grind the coating 4 inches around the damage. This will assure that the body filler will not be applied over paint. Once ground, blow the repair area with compressed air.

Additional Resources

I have many additional resources that will be included at the end of this book. However, I do not want to include them under each chapter. As an instructor, I am aware that too much is not always a good thing. Information overload may leave you feeling behind, confused, and/or burned-out. Therefore, concentrate on the information and resources in each module. Once you have completed the book, you can explore the additional resources. Again, don't stress about getting through all of the additional resources all at once. Remember simplicity...keep it simple.

Module 3 Quiz Metal Straightening

Once you have completed the module content, take the module 3 quiz below. Please note that you must score 75% or higher to receive a certificate. This quiz has 21 questions. There is not a time limit set on this quiz so take your time. Find the correct answer if you do not know for sure. **The objective of this quiz is to help you learn the** information if you do not know the answer, not guessing. Good luck!

MODULE 4 BODY FILLERS

"Body Fillers, Glaze, Fiberglass"

Body filler is used to fill small imperfections on vehicle body parts. Once a dent has been repaired there are still small imperfections that will need to be filled and smoothed to produce the same smooth shape that the part was in before the accident. This module is going to explain how to properly prepare the surface and apply body filler. Once cleaned and the damage has been repaired, you are ready to apply body filler.

Grind 4 inches past damaged area - cross grind the metal with 24 to 50 grit. The damaged area is repaired and now ready for body filler. You do not want to apply any body filler over paint. Therefore, if you need to extend your grind area, do this now. Remember, you want at least 4 inches past your repair area. This should provide enough space to spread the filler without applying the filler on top of the paint. Care should be taken not to over grind. This could thin or overheat the metal. Once you have the surface ground and ready for filler, do not touch the metal with your hands, as the oils on your hands could cause inadequate adhesion.

Mix the Body Filler
Use a nonporous surface and a plastic or metal spreader to mix your filler. Do not use cardboard to mix filler on. Cardboard will absorb some of the

resins in the filler. You can use plastic, steel, or any other surface that is not porous. Next, open the can of body filler. If it is separated, it will need to be mixed. You can do this by using a paint stick. The cream hardener will also need to be kneaded. You can do this by squeezing the tube with your fingers, which mixes the hardener inside of the tube. Next, put the amount of filler needed on the mixing board. For every golf ball size of filler use about a dime size of hardener. Now you can mix the two parts together. Do not stir or whip when mixing. This will cause air bubbles, which will lead to severe pinholes. Mix the filler in one direction, by folding and spreading in one direction. Be certain the filler is mixed thoroughly. You want one uniform color. If you can see streaks in the filler, keep mixing.

Apply the filler to repair area

Now you can use a plastic or metal spreader to apply the filler. You only have 5 to 10 minutes to apply the filler. You want to put your first coat on tight by pushing your spreader hard against the surface. This will push the filler tight into the ground scratches producing superior adhesion. It is better to apply several thin coats, rather than trying to fill it in one thick coat. Sometimes one application is enough, but don't be afraid to apply a second or third coat if needed. However, don't exceed 1/4 inch of combined layers of filler thickness. Be sure to sand between coats to identify low areas. If you have filler remaining after application it must be thrown away. Never try to put leftover filler back in the can. It will ruin the entire can of filler.

Block Sanding Body Filler

The best advice that I can give you when sanding body filler is to cross sand and do not over sand the filler. Those are the two most common mistakes that I see. Bigger repair areas start out by sanding with 36 grit and then switching to 80 grit to minimize the 36 grit scratches. Guide coat can be used at any time to help determine highs and lows. If there are pinholes or small imperfections, a coat of finish glaze can be applied and blocked with 150 grit. If it does not need finish glaze, finish the body filler by sanding with 150 grit. One more tip. The coarser the sandpaper, the better it levels. The smoother the sandpaper, the more it begins to polish and follow the contour. Therefore, be certain that the filler is level before switching to the smoother grits. Switching to a smooth grit too soon may result in a lumpy finish.

Finishing Glaze

Finishing glaze does not have to be used, but it does have many benefits and can make the job much easier. Glaze is a thinner filler that spreads smoother and works well as your final coat. Glaze should not be applied too thick as it is designed to fill pinholes and minor scratches and imperfections. In addition to spreading smoother, glaze can also be applied over sanded body filler, sanded paint, sanded primer, or metal. This makes it excellent to apply over the entire repair area, including the sanded paint.

Finishing Glaze on Hail Damage

Another advantage of using finish glaze is when repairing small hail dents. Since glaze can be applied over sanded paint, it is not necessary to remove all of the paint to the metal. Simply sand the dent area with 180 grit, clean, apply glaze, and block out. This is quicker and you do not have to remove any of the factory e-coat, which is the superior corrosion resistant coating.

This covers dent repair. Now it's ready to featheredge, which we're going to cover, on the refinish side. Let's discuss other fillers that may be required.

Fiberglass Filler

What Is Fiberglass?

Raw fiberglass comes in a soft fabric like material. When saturated with liquid resin and hardener, it becomes hard and very strong. There are not too many fiberglass auto parts on modern day cars, as they have all started using other composites like SMC and carbon fiber. However, fiberglass was used on early model corvettes, truck hoods, and many other parts. There are still aftermarket parts that are manufactured from fiberglass and it is still used for boats and jet skis.

The Difference Between Fiberglass and Fiberglass Filler

Fiberglass filler comes in a can and is mixed with a cream hardener. It mixes a lot like regular body filler, but it is thicker and a little harder to mix. The filler has fiberglass mixed in it. It comes in short hair and long hair. This is the length of the fiberglass that is mixed in the filler. Both provide excellent waterproof properties as they do not absorb moisture. Both fiberglass fillers are stronger than regular body filler. The long hair filler provides the most strength out of the two. However, these fillers are very difficult to sand. The filler is also thick, which makes it hard to level and smooth like regular body filler.

Why Use Fiberglass Filler If It's So Difficult To Sand?

The reason we use fiberglass filler in auto body repair is not really for the added strength, but for the waterproof properties. It is recommended to apply a thin layer of fiberglass filler over any welding that is performed. Body filler absorbs moisture, which will lead to corrosion and rust. By using the fiberglass, we eliminate the moisture absorption problem. Since our main purpose is to seal the welded area, the short hair fiberglass is sufficient for the application.

What Fiberglass Filler Can Be Used On

This filler can be used over bare metal or fiberglass.

Finishing The Repair

As I mentioned, fiberglass does not sand well. That is why I recommend only applying a small amount to the welded areas and rough sanding it using 36 grit. After this is done, you can apply body filler on the top of the fiberglass filler and finish the repair as you normally would using body filler.

Warning

You should always wear proper protective equipment when sanding any filler. However, extreme caution should be taken when sanding fiberglass products. It not only itches and irritates your skin, but it is extremely unhealthy to breathe the fiberglass. Be certain to wear an approved dust respiration, gloves, and eye protection, and you may even want to wear a disposable paint suit. If some of the fiberglass does get on your skin, take a cold shower. This will help keep your pores small and allow the fiberglass to wash off.

Tip

One tip to speed up the sanding process is to sand the filler before it has fully cured. By sanding in the green state, the filler is much softer and sands much faster. This technique should only be used to level the filler. Do not sand too much during this stage, as you will undercut the filler.

If you are not a fan of fiberglass filler or if it irritates your skin, there is an alternative filler that can be used. This filler is called All Metal, which is an aluminum based filler, which has the same waterproofing properties.

Module 4 Resources

Visit www.TeachMeHow.info and sign into the members website to access the resources below.

Audios
•Module 4 Text Podcast

Videos
1.   •Applying Body Filler
2.   •Block Sanding Body Filler
3.   •Applying Finish Glaze
4.   •Applying Body Filler 3M
5.   •Applying Finish Glaze 3M
6.   •Fiberglass Filler
7.   •Q&A - Why The Gloves

PowerPoints
1.   •No PowerPoints for this module

Product Information
1.   •All-Metal Filler
2.   •Body Filler
3.   •Body Filler 3M
4.   •Finish Glaze
5.   •Finish Glaze 3M - Trouble locating online - Check TPC
6.   •Fiberglass Filler

7. •Mixing Boards and Spreaders
8. •Blocks
9. •Guide Coat

Product Technical Sheet

1. •All-Metal Filler
2. •Body Filler
3. •Body Filler 3M
4. •Finish Glaze
5. •Finish Glaze 3M
6. •3M Dynamic Mixing System
7. •Fiberglass Filler
8. •Guide Coat

MSDS

1. •All Metal Filler
2. •Body Filler 3M
3. •Finish Glaze
4. •Finish Glaze 3M
5. •Fiberglass Filler
6. •Guide Coat

Websites

- **No Websites For This Module**

Module 4 Training Activity

Read the text and watch all videos. Be sure to read all product technical data sheets to become familiar

with them and how to properly use each product.
Notice how they may vary from company to
company, but provide the necessary information.
Read and watch first, then use the step by step as a
memory jogger. On your junk panels, start to apply
body filler and block sand. **Body filler must be
applied to metal. However, there is one
alternative method. That is by spraying the
repair area with epoxy primer first. I do not use
that method, but it does have benefits,
especially for restoration work. Why do you
think this method may be beneficial? Post in
Q&A section.** Lastly, complete module 4 quiz.

Step-By-Step
1.   •If the repair has been welded, mix and
     apply fiberglass filler to repair area.
2.   •Sand the filler with 36 grit. There is no
     need to use a finer grit as body fill will be
     applied over the fiberglass. All you need is to
     level the glass filler.
3.   •Mix and apply body filler over the repair
     area. Cover and extend body filler over
     fiberglass. Do not extend the filler onto the
     paint surface.
4.   •Block sand (cross sand) the filler with 36
     grit sandpaper. (This step can be done before

the filler is completely dry to reduce the amount of sanding required.)

5. •Repeat step if there are still lows.

6. •Allow to fully cure (15 to 20 minutes) and spray with guide coat.

7. •Block sand (cross sand) with 80 grit sandpaper. Sand just enough to remove guide coat. If guide coat does not sand off in an area, this indicates a low and additional filler will be needed.

8. •Optional: Either apply guide coat and block sand with 150 grit; or, apply a coat of finish glaze over entire repair area. Remember, glaze can be applied over sanded paint too.

9. •Finish filler or glaze by blocking with 150 grit.

Now the body work is complete. Next, we're going to touch on welding, plastic, then jump into the refinish side of the repairs.

Additional Resources

I have many additional resources that will be included at the end of this book. However, I do not want to include them under each chapter. As an instructor, I am aware that too much is not always a good thing. Information overload may leave you feeling behind, confused, and/or burned-out. Therefore, concentrate on the information and resources in each module. Once you have completed the book, you can explore the additional resources. Again, don't stress about getting through all of the additional resources all at once. Remember simplicity...keep it simple.

Module 4 Body Fillers Quiz

Once you have completed the module content, take the module 4 quiz below. Please note that you must score 75% or higher to receive a certificate. This quiz has 23 questions. There is not a time limit set on this quiz so take your time. Find the correct answer if you do not know for sure. **The objective of this quiz is to help you learn the information if you do not know the answer, not guessing. Good luck!**

MODULE 5 WELDING

"When You Catch A Baseball For The First Time, Do You Stop Practicing?"

Learning How To Weld In Auto Body Repair

Vehicles consists of many parts that are attached in a variety of ways. One of the methods used is welds. Therefore, a technician must master welding to become a professional collision repair technician.

Most Common Welds From Factory

Most of the welds from the factory consist of spot welds. This is a machine that compresses the pieces of metal together and then a high voltage spot welds the two pieces together. In this process, there is no additional filler metal used to complete the weld process, which does not add any additional weight to the vehicle, as nuts and bolts would.

Welding In The Auto Body Shops

Collision repair shops have machines that will produce spot welds as well, but many of the areas that need to be repaired are hard to get to, which may require an alternative welding method. The welding method used in this situation is called a plug weld. This is done by punching an 8 mm hole in the top piece of metal, much like a hole in a piece of notebook paper and placing it on top of the piece of metal to be welded. Once clamped in place, simply weld the hole with a MIG welder while getting good penetration into the bottom piece. Sounds easy enough? Well, it is easy to learn, but hours need to be spent perfecting these welds before making actual welds on a car. Just like in baseball, you don't stop throwing and catching as soon as you learn how. No, you keep on practicing to become better and better. Well, if you don't practice catching you may just miss the ball, but if you don't have the welding down, your welds may not hold up in an accident, which could lead to unnecessary injuries.

There are many other types of welds, but I just wanted to touch on plug welds and the importance of practicing first. So get your welder back out, punch some holes in metal coupons, and weld them to another coupon. Repeat, repeat, then do it again!

Types of Welds Used in Auto Body
There are basically three types of welds used in auto body repair. Plug welds, as we've already mentioned, and we also have butt welds, which may or may not have a backing plate, and a lap weld.

A butt weld is used when sectioning parts together. This is achieved by butting the two pieces of metal together so that they are flush and level. This will allow you to grind the weld when completed so the weld can be filled and smoothed out without the repair being visible. This is when you would use the fiberglass filler over the welded area.

A lap weld is when one piece of metal laps over the other piece of metal. You may need to do this type of weld when replacing structural parts that recommend this weld type. These welds are normally in areas that do not require an invisible repair. Therefore, the fiberglass and body filler are not required. However, you may need to apply seam sealer to properly seal the area to prevent moisture and corrosion.

There is a lot to cover in welding. We are not going to cover it all in this book, but I am going to highlight a few of the important steps. I have prepared several audios that are helpful and my students have prepared a few videos explaining the different types of welds. I have also included another video from Motorz that I think is useful to help you teach yourself how to weld. In addition to the audios and videos, I also recommend visiting the online training offered by

Lincoln and Miller. They have a lot of useful tips as well.

The most important thing to do is to practice. Welding takes much practice. Get your welder out and some scrap metal about the thickness of body sheet metal. Then just <u>practice, practice, practice.</u>

One last thing that I would like to mention. When you are actually welding a panel or patch onto a car you may not be able to get back into the enclosed area that you are welding. You cannot use regular primer to protect the metal as it would burn off by the heat of welding. However, they make a product called weld-thru primer that can be used. Simply spray inside of the area that you will be welding. The zinc-rich primer will not be destroyed by the heat and the metal will be protected and promote corrosion protection.

Module 5 Resources

Visit www.TeachMeHow.info and sign into the members website to access the resources below.

Audio
1.   •Module 5 Text Podcast
2.   •Oxy/Acetylene
3.   •Mig Welding Part 1
4.   •Mig Welding Part 2
5.   •Mig Welding Part 3
6.   •Mig Welding Part 4
7.   •Mig Welding Part 5

Videos
1.   •Changing Gas Bottle and Set-up
2.   •Plug Weld
3.   •Butt Weld
4.   •Lap Weld
5.   •Learning To Weld 101
6.   •Weld Through Primer

PowerPoints
1.   •MIG Welding

Product Information
1.   •Lincoln Mig Welding

2. •.023 Wire
3. •Shielding Gas - 75% Argon - 25% CO_2 - You may also be able to rent these from your local welding store.
4. •Weld Thru Primer

Product Technical Sheet

1. •MIG WELDER
2. •.023 Page 6
3. •Shielding Gas Page 8
4. •Weld Thru Primer

MSDS

1. •Shielding Gas
2. •Weld Thru Primer

Websites

1. •Miller E-Training
2. •Lincoln E-Training

Module 5 Training Activity

There are enough resources here to keep you busy quite some time. I included audio, video, product information and technical data, MSDS, and e-training though Miller and Lincoln. First read the module text, listen to audios, and watch the videos. Then visit the e-training and complete all of the intro and MIG welding process. They both have great training, which can give you a better understanding of the welding process. However, welding takes practice. If you have a welder or know someone who does, get some scrap metal and start welding. You can probably go to any body shop and ask them for junk body parts to practice on.

First learn how to set up and adjust your welder. Remember, you want a constant buzz sound. Kind of like bacon frying. Next, grind metal and weld beads. Once you get good at running beads, practice the three different type of welds. When you become good at that start welding in different positions, as you may have to do on a car. Flat, vertical, horizontal, and the hardest, overhead. Again, this takes a lot of practice so take your time.

Many car parts now have a galvanized coating from the factory. What extra precautions should you take when welding galvanized steel? Post in the Q&A section.

Step-By-Step

1.   •There are many different types of welds, different positions, and different reasons for welding (patch, sectioning, frame, unibody,

new panels, etc.). Therefore, it is hard to provide a step-by-step process. However, that will all come with time and practice. So I'll say it again....just practice for now.

Additional Resources

I have many additional resources that will be included at the end of this book. However, I do not want to include them under each chapter. As an instructor, I am aware that too much is not always a good thing. Information overload may leave you feeling behind, confused, and/or burned-out. Therefore, concentrate on the information and resources in each module. Once you have completed the book, you can explore the additional resources. Again, don't stress about getting through all of the additional resources all at once. Remember simplicity...keep it simple.

Module 5 Welding Quiz

Once you have completed the module content, take the module 5 quiz below. Please note that you must score 75% or higher to receive a certificate. This quiz has 24 questions. There is not a time limit set on this quiz so take your time. Find the correct answer if you do not know for sure. **The objective of this quiz is to help you learn the**

information if you do not know the answer, not guessing. Good luck!

MODULE 6 PLASTIC REPAIR
"Like It Or Not, It's Here To Stay"

We used to just replace most plastic parts, but that time has passed. As more plastics are being used, advanced repair methods and products have been developed. We just need to make sure technicians know how to use the new products to properly make the repairs.

That is what this module is all about.....plastics and plastic repair.

Plastic Repair - Like It Or Not, It's Here To Stay

A Different World

The collision repair industry is changing fast. Not too long ago cars were not built with much plastic. Mostly interior parts, but even much of the inside of a car was made with metal. In the past 15 to 20 years, plastics and composites have became widely used for interior, exterior, body parts, mechanical parts, etc. Plastic is not going anywhere, so we need to learn how to repair it properly.

Why Plastic?

The government started pushing car makers to make cars more fuel efficient. One obvious solution was to make the car lighter. This is when car makers started working with metal and other materials to reduce weight in vehicles. Lighter metal started being designed, such as high strength steel to allow the metal to have equivalent strength with much thinner metal. At the same time, engineers started brainstorming and started using lightweight plastic for many of the parts that were made of steel. Apparently, the results were positive, as there is more plastic in each new body style of cars.

More Fuel Economy

To this day the government is requiring car makers to meet certain requirements in order to sell cars in the U.S. Therefore, the automakers are going to do whatever it takes to make this happen. I believe we will see more plastic, aluminum, carbon fiber, and other composites in the years to come.

Like It Or Hate It

There are many technicians who do not like working with plastics. However, whether we like it or not, the fact that it is here to stay is a pretty safe bet. I am not trying to promote the use of plastic, but we do need to teach technicians how to properly repair it.

New Methods

With all the plastics, companies such as 3M have developed some awesome products to repair plastic.

There are a few folks out there who may prefer to use a plastic welding method, but the adhesive products have really made this a simple process. Sure, there are different concerns for repairing plastics than repairing metal, but when plastic is repaired properly, it's as good as new.

Types of Plastic

Thermoset plastic: (wikipedia) is basically a product that consists of several parts together that become one. In other words, thermoset plastic changes chemical properties during the curing process. Like body filler, once the two products are mixed together and dried, it is now a different product. You are not going to be able to separate the body filler and hardener again. One of the things that you need to remember about thermoset plastic is that it does not reshape easily, if at all, with heat.

Thermoplastics: (wikipedia) are more flexible and did not take a chemical change during production of the part. It is kind of like latex paint. It is the same product dry or wet. In the dry state it simply means that the water has evaporated from the paint. Therefore, the two products are separated after they were mixed together. Thermoplastic is easy to reshape with applied heat.

Below are audios that explain the different ways to repair plastic.

Module 6 Resources

Visit www.TeachMeHow.info and sign into the members website to access the resources below.

Audio
1.   •Module 6 Text Podcast
2.   •Audio 1
3.   •Audio 2
4.   •Audio 3
5.   •Audio 4

Videos
1.   •Plastic Welding 1
2.   •Plastic Welding 2
3.   •Plastic Welding 3
4.   •Thermoplastic
5.   •Thermoset Plastic

PowerPoints
1.   •Plastics

Product Information
1. •Plastic Welding Machine
2. •3M Flexible Parts Repair
3. •Adhesion Promoter
4. •3" Grinder
5. •3" Grinder 50 grit
6. •DA Sander
7. •80 Grit DA Sandpaper
8. •180 Grit DA Sandpaper

Product Technical Sheet
1. •3M Flexible Parts Repair
2. •Adhesion Promoter

MSDS
1. •3M Flexible Parts Repair
2. •Adhesion Promoter

Websites
1. •Plastic 1 Sided Repair - Online Training - with Quiz
2. •Plastic 2 Sided Repair - Online Training - with Quiz
3. •Tab Repair - Online Training - with Quiz

Module 6 Training Activity
Read the module text, then listen to the audio podcasts. Then watch the videos and read the

technical data sheets. I also have two 3M training lessons for you to complete. In the 3M training it will ask for company and title. **You can put Collision Blast Training for the company and put Student for job title**. You will also be able to print certificates upon successful completion of each lesson. Once you can completed the content, visit a body shop to ask for a scrap bumper cover if you don't already have one. I would perform a practice repair on a part that does not need to be used for a car. Plastic repair is fairly easy and you should have the hang of it after several repairs.

Lastly, there is a module 6 quiz, but I kept it small since you have taken 3 additional quizzes in this module.

Step-By-Step

1.   •Wash plastic part with soap and water.
2.   •Clean part with a plastic cleaner to assure all contaminates are removed.
3.   •Using a 3" grinder with 50 grit sandpaper, grind several inches past the damaged area.
4.   •Using a 3" grinder with 50 grit sandpaper, dish the front side of the damaged part. Once damaged is dished out, grind an additional two to three inches past the damaged area. As with metal, you do not want adhesive applied over paint.

5. •Using a DA sander with 80 grit, sand the edges of the front of repair area, then follow with 180 grit sandpaper to feather edge the repair on the front side.

6. •Blow front and back with compressed air to clean surface.

7. •Apply 1 - 2 thin coats of adhesion promoter. Allow to dry 5 minutes or recommended time as stated by brand.

8. •Apply tape to the front side to prevent adhesive from dripping out.

9. •Apply a tight coat of adhesive to the back side.

10. •Cut and apply reinforced fiber and apply another coat of adhesive on the top.

11. •Allow to set up.

12. •Remove tape and apply adhesive on the front side, a tight coat followed by a fill coat.

13. •Allow to dry and sand with block or DA with 80 grit sandpaper.

14. •Apply Guide Coat and sand with 180 grit to remove all 80 grit scratches.

15. •If there are still lows this process may need to be repeated, however, if it is a small imperfection or pinhole, flexible parts putty may be applied and sanded.

Additional Resources

I have many additional resources that will be included at the end of this book. However, I do not want to include them under each chapter. As an instructor, I am aware that too much is not always a good thing. Information overload may leave you feeling behind, confused, and/or burned-out. Therefore, concentrate on the information and resources in each module. Once you have completed the book, you can explore the additional resources. Again, don't stress about getting through all of the additional resources all at once. Remember simplicity...keep it simple.

Module 6 Plastic Repair Quiz

Once you have completed the module content, take the module 6 quiz below. Please note that you must score 75% or higher to receive a certificate. This quiz is short because you have the 3 additional quizzes above. There are only 8 questions. There is not a time limit set on this quiz so take your time. Find the correct answer if you do not know for sure. **The objective of this quiz is to help you learn the information if you do not know the answer, not guessing**. Good luck!

MODULE 7 PREPARATION

"It All Starts Here"

Featheredging, Masking, Primer, Block Sanding, Final Sanding

One of the most important, or perhaps the most important, thing you need to do when painting a car is to properly prep it. Without proper preparation, the rest is useless. It's like an iceberg...you see about 10% to 20% of it sticking out of the water. However, what you don't see is the other 80% to 90% that is underneath the water. Well, in painting, we see the paint, the finished product. However 80% + of that awesome paint job is due to what you can't see, the hours of prep.

It is a common mistake to rush through the prep step, then try your hardest to paint like a pro. However, that just don't work. It's just like trying your hardest on a test that you did not study for. No matter how hard you try on test day, you're not going to do well without learning the information first.

In this module, we are going to focus on cleaning......that must be important as I keep bringing it up. I hope to have this etched into your mind by the end of this book. We're also going to focus on featheredging, block sanding, final sanding, and once again, cleaning before putting it in the paint booth.

Did I say that proper cleaning is important? I am going to start this module off with that.

The Professional Paint Job Is Not About A Fancy Paint Gun

All the awesome auto paint colors are what make cars look great and attract interest from car enthusiasts around the world. Ed Roth broke the mold by altering the stock look with modified body parts, pinstripes, and custom paint. Since then people began customizing cars in every way imaginable. This has created a lot of people's interest in custom painting. However, the same rule applied then and still applies today, which is, it does not start with the paint gun, it starts with the wash mitt.

As a collision repair instructor, I see the same thing many times when it come to painting a car. Students tend to rush through the preparation stage and then expect superior end results. Painting is an art and it does take practice. Travel speed, distance, spray pattern overlap, and technique is necessary to learn to produce professional results, but more attention needs to be concentrated on preparing the car for paint than the spraying itself.

Here is an example that I give my students when I am trying to convey this point. Let's say that we did not properly wash and clean the vehicle. Then we sanded the car, but fast and sloppy. Lastly, we slap a little tape and paper to mask it off. If Chip Foose (very known for his painting abilities) came in and painted the car, how would it turn out? Well, it would have dirt in it as we rushed through the preparation process, probably fish eyes in the paint, paint over spray on the glass and moldings where paint seeped through. Well, I guess you could say it would look horrible. The paint would probably peel later due to a loss of adhesion. All of Foose's abilities are useless if the car is not prepped correctly. This is similar to spending $200,000 building a nice home on top of a bad foundation. Even if you use the best materials to build the house, it will fall apart if the foundation is not right. Therefore, assuring that you have a good foundation is important before building a home, just like having a properly prepped car before painting it.

I know that I stress that point, but it is often overlooked. So get your wash mitt out and spend extra time washing the car before starting repairs. Then take your time and ensure that all the surface to be painted is sanded so the top coating will properly adhere. Always re-clean the area to remove all dirt. Dirt in crevices may blow out with the air pressure of the paint gun and get in the paint job, if you do not blow the car off thoroughly before masking it off. Use a good quality paper and masking tape to protect glass and the other items that you do not want painted. Wipe the surface with quality wax and grease remover to remove all traces of contaminations, waxes, silicones, etc. Use a tack rag to remove final dirt and lint before applying the paint coatings. Now you can start spraying the car. Spend 80% of your time and efforts becoming a good prepper and 20% of your time perfecting your spraying techniques. This is what it takes to produce a professional paint job that will look great and turn heads.

Now that we have that out of the way, let's continue in our repair process.

Featheredging
After the body work has been completed and finished with 150 grit sandpaper, many shops send it from the body shop to the paint shop. However, there are many variations of how shop owners like

to divide this, but traditionally, after being blocked with 150, it's sent to the painter.

The first thing a painter will need to do before priming and painting is to prep the repair area. The block left 150 grit scratches on the filler and surrounding area. There may also be grinding marks and edges where the paint coatings meet the metal. To smooth the paint edges out and the other scratches, you will need to featheredge. This is done using a dual action sander with 220 grit sandpaper. This the one and only exception that you can tilt the DA on its edge. This will help you make the transition from paint to metal easier. You want to bevel each layer of paint or primer at least ¼ inch. It will look like you have rings around your repair area. Each ring should vary from ¼" +. If this is not properly done, the rings may show up after the car has been painted.

Sanding

Now that the featheredging is completed, we can sand everything else that is going to be painted. But why do we sand? Many people think it's to provide a smooth surface, but it's actually the opposite. We are actually roughing the surface up so the paint will stick. Think about painting a piece of glass. It is pretty easy to imagine the paint peeling off as the glass is so smooth. End result....sanding provides adhesion to prevent peeling.

Mechanical Adhesion

Primer and/or paint will not adhere to an un-sanded panel. The surface must be roughed up, which will produce a mechanical adhesion. Not properly preparing the surface will result in loss of adhesion and peeling. Most paint starts peeling from an edge, so make certain special attention to edges is taken.

No Hard Edges

Once the body filler or glaze putty is block sanded with 150 grit and featheredged with 220 it is now ready for primer. The first thing that you need to do is mask the adjacent panels and areas that you do not want to get primer to get on. This sounds simple enough, but many mistakes are made doing this. One of the common mistakes is making hard edges with the primer. This is done by masking a square around the damaged area. During the priming process, primer is sprayed against the tape edge causing a hard edge. This creates additional work trying to feather the primer edge smooth. We'll explain how to prevent that and other common mistakes shortly. Before we discuss masking, let's discuss prepping the panel before masking and priming.

When Painting The Entire Panel

Before you start priming and masking, prepare the entire panel for paint or clear coat. First, sand several inches around the repair area with 320 grit on a DA sander. (This is the featheredge area we just discussed.) If the entire panel is going to be painted, go ahead and sand the entire panel with 500 grit on a DA sander. (You can also hand sand.) Make certain that when final sanding with a DA that you use the interface pad. Once the panel is sanded with a DA sander or by hand with 400 to 500 grit, use a red scuff pad to scuff the edges and all other areas that are hard to get with a DA sander. Do not rush this step, as edges are very important. If paint or primer is going to peel, it usually starts from an edge. Once you have the panel completely sanded, clean the surface with compressed air and wipe the panel with wax and grease remover. Go ahead and clean surrounding areas where tape may be applied to ensure the tape will adhere properly.

Blending Within A Panel

What if you're blending within a panel? Blending within a panel is where you are only going to paint the repair area and not the entire panel. This still requires sanding to the entire panel, as the entire panel will need to be clear coated. This uses the same methods, but you must use finer grit sandpapers. Now I just want to give you a heads-up on how to do this, but do not get stressed about blending. We'll cover that later.

To repair a blend within a panel for primer, sand past the repair area with 320 grit using a DA with an inter surface pad. Sand several inches past your repair area. Then switch to 500 grit DA using the inter surface pad and sand an additional 2-4 inches past the repair area. Now switch to 800 grit sandpaper using a DA with inter surface pad to sand the remaining panel surface. Once the entire panel is sanded, use a gray, make sure it is gray, not red, scuff pad to scuff the edges and hard-to-reach areas of the panel. Now you're ready to clean the surface as explained above. Blow with compressed air and wipe with wax and grease remover.

Eliminate Peeling
By sanding the entire panel before priming, you will ensure that all primer will adhere properly. If your primer sprays out a little further than you intended, you will be safe, as it has already been sanded. I have seen primer applied over un-sanded paint

before. If left like this, it will cause the primer and whatever is applied over the primer (paint and clear) to peel off with it. That is something that you definitely do not want to happen.

Now that the panel is repaired and prepped, you can get it ready to mask and prime.

Masking

The repair area has been repaired and finish sanded with 150 grit sandpaper, featheredged and the panel prepped for primer. Now it is time to get some primer on the repair area.

Take Time To Save Time

The purpose of masking is to prevent primer over spray from getting on the areas that it is not intended to be. With the types of primers used today, it is necessary to take all measures to make certain that over spray does not get onto the unintended surfaces. First, the two-part epoxy and urethane primers are very difficult to remove. Back when we used to use lacquer primer, all the over spray could be cleaned with a little thinner on a rag. However, today's catalyzed primers do not wipe off. Once the primer is dried on the surface, you can rub with thinner all day long without getting it all the way off. The second reason is that these primers carry a long distance. Again, with the old lacquer primer, if it traveled more than 12 inches it would be dust by the time it landed on the surface. However, the primers of today can travel the full length of the vehicle and still stick to the painted surface, glass, moldings, etc. With this said, more care should be taken to properly mask a vehicle for primer. The extra time spent properly masking a repair area for primer will save you much time rubbing, sanding, and buffing to remove unnecessary overspray.

No More, No Less

You need to be certain to primer everything that needs to be primed. That is any metal, filler, or scratches made by the 150 - 220 grit sanding. However, there is no need to prime anything else. For example, if you have a 6" diameter repair area, there is no need to primer the entire or even half of the panel. This is something that I have noticed some students tend to do. You only need to prime the repaired area. The spray will slightly exceed the repair area, but try to keep it small as possible. Another thing to remember is to keep primer out of areas that it does not need to be. For example, molding edges and jambs. There is nothing sloppier than to open a car door after it has been completed and see primer overspray, or to see primer on the edge of a molding. The reason this happens is because many times when masking for primer, the person masking thinks, well, this is just for priming and rushes through the masking process. Then when masking to paint, more care and attention to detail is taken. You may not have paint on the unwanted areas, but you have primer, which looks even worse than the paint would have. So be certain to take as much pride in masking the vehicle for priming as you do for getting it ready for paint.

When masking off jambs, mask to the edge of the panel. There is no need to allow any primer into the jamb area. Therefore the edge of your tape should be at the edge of the panel to prevent over spray from getting into the jamb area. Now when we mask for painting, we will mask back from the edge slightly to allow a little overspray to spray onto the jamb. This eliminates noticeable lines, but for now, mask right on the edge of the panel.

Nothing Hard About It
The only hard edges you should have when priming are the jamb edges. You should try to avoid all other edges if possible. Hard edges are a definite "no-no." Let's take the same 6 inch diameter repair

area and mask an 8 inch square around it. You only get primer where you want it, but now you have hard edges to featheredge out. Let's look at another approach to mask the 6 inch repair area. Mask all adjacent panels and anything near the repair area that you do not want primer on. Then you can go out 12" and back mask if needed. Back masking is the process of masking something and flipping the paper over, creating a smoother edge. When correct, the paper will now have the bottom side of the paper facing up. For instance, if the top of the paper is blue and the bottom of the paper is white, now the white will be showing. Now that we have it back masked, we still do not need to spray primer all the way to the paper. Try to avoid that if possible. Ideally, try not to have any edges at all. The over spray makes an easy area to sand with as little effort as possible.

If In Doubt...Cover It

Over spray is something that you do not want to get on unwanted surfaces. So must the entire car be covered? The answer is, if in doubt, cover it. It only takes a few minutes to unroll plastic and cover the car. If we take the 6 inch diameter repair area and mask around it using 18 inch paper and set the spray gun using low pressure, you may be all right. However, just a little over spray can cause you hours of cleanup and grief. This is something that you need to get a feel for, but if in doubt, bag the car with plastic. If you're priming the entire panel, be certain to cover the entire car with plastic. A little time spent in the front end will save much time in the back end.

Tell-Tale Signs

Masking is perceived by amateurs as being unskilled and unimportant. However, I think you will agree that the best looking paint job can look horrible if you see paint and/or primer on moldings or in jambs. The idea is to make invisible repairs. Improper masking is the easiest and fastest way to determine that a vehicle has been repainted.

We're masked and ready to prime. So let's discuss primers.

Priming the Repair Area - Why Prime and What

Types of Primer to Use

What Is Primer?

According to Wikipedia, "primer is a preparatory coating put on materials before painting. Priming ensures better adhesion of paint to the surface, increases paint durability, and provides additional protection for the material being painted. The term primer comes from the Latin word primus meaning first because it precedes the other coatings."

Adhesion Is Key, But There is More

Adhesion is a key reason to use primer. However, in automotive primers, it also provides corrosion protection too. Therefore, a primer that provides both good adhesion and corrosion protection is needed. I recommend using an epoxy primer to provide these needs. Most epoxies can be applied on most types of substrates and is compatible with most top coats. Some technicians prefer etch primer to apply on bare metal to provide good adhesion. Etch primer has a high acid content that bites into the metal, but does not have the corrosion protection like epoxy does. I will talk about when etching primer in an aerosol can come in handy in a little bit.

Mixing Epoxy - It's Like The First Day Of Class

We use PPG and Shopline (a line of PPG) products, but other brands may have similar directions. Be sure to read the manufacturer's procedure page to determine what they recommend. However, many epoxies have an induction time. This is an amount of time the two chemicals need to be mixed together before using. It's like going to a new town or your first day of class. You're quiet and nervous until you get to know the people around you. Once you get to know everyone, you feel much more comfortable. After mixing the catalyst with the epoxy primer, the chemical needs a little time to accept each other as well. It may only be 15 to 20 minutes, but be sure to read the procedure page for the specific product to know for sure.

Spraying The Primer

According to the new 6H rule, all primer needs to be sprayed inside an approved spray area. If you're priming a small area, you may consider lowering the fluid, narrowing the fan pattern, and turning the air pressure down. This will allow you to spray a smaller area with less over spray. Be certain to cover all areas that were sanded with 220 grit or coarser. Apply two medium wet coats to the repair area. Remember not to spray primer all the way to your masking paper. Keeping the primer area as small as possible will provide the easiest repair.

Flash Time - Don't Even Think About Passing Go

Flash time is the amount of time that is needed between coats. Rushing the flash time throughout the car refinish process is something I see often, which results in many different problems. Each coat must have time to flash to allow all the solvents to evaporate. If you apply another coat before the primer has flashed off, it will trap the solvent and cause a number of problems. Loss of adhesion and solvent popping are a few of the most common problems. You must also realize that the time given in the procedure page is probably around 70 degrees. If it is 50 degrees in the shop at the time you spray the primer, then flash time must be extended. One coat at a time. No double coats or rushing the flash times. You've spent a lot of time on the repair; don't blow it now.

Primer Surfacer - The Final Fill

The Purpose

Primer surfacer is the final step or your final chance to produce the perfect surface with the correct texture before painting. Scratches and small imperfections can be repaired with this fill primer. Filling is the main purpose of this type of primer; you can think of it as a final filler. We finished the body filler or glazing putty with 150 grit, featheredged, cleaned the surface, masked, applied two coats of epoxy, and now we're ready to apply primer surfacer.

Flash and Window Times

After the epoxy has been applied, you can now apply the primer surfacer. Be certain to allow the epoxy to flash the recommended amount of time. The manufacturer's procedure page will tell you how long of a flash time needed before top coating. With PPG you need to let it flash at least 30 minutes. However, you also have a window. This is the time that you have to apply another coat without sanding. Most epoxies have a long window time. The epoxy that I am familiar with has a 72 hour window. If you wait more than 72 hours to apply the primer surfacer, it must be lightly scuffed to ensure proper adhesion.

Adhesion - Mechanical vs Chemical

I keep talking about adhesion. I would like to expand on this and tell you why this is important. Adhesion is just another word for stick-to. For instance, in upcoming lessons we will refer to glue as adhesives. To prevent body filler, primer, paint, etc. from peeling, it needs to adhere to the surface. There are two ways to provide adhesion. The first is a mechanical adhesion. This is why we sand the surface before we apply the coating. That is why it is so important to sand the edges extremely well. If a panel is going to peel, chances are it will start peeling from an edge. The second type of adhesion is chemical adhesion. This is when there is still a chemical bond with two products. For example, the 72 hour window with the epoxy primer is the time the surface will produce the chemical bond. After that, the chemical bond will no longer adhere. That is why after the 72 hour window, the surface will need to be re-sanded. Since we no longer have the chemical adhesion, we now have the mechanical adhesion to takes its place.

Applying The Primer Surfacer

All right, I took a little rabbit trail, but I wanted to make sure that you understand flash times, window times, and the types of adhesion. Now, let's talk about applying the primer surfacer. After the epoxy has flashed off the recommended amount of time, apply your first coat of primer surfacer. Only apply enough to cover the epoxy primer. Check the procedure page to determine the recommended number of coats needed to achieve the desired thickness or mils. Normally, two to three coats are sufficient. I usually apply two wet coats allowing each coat to flash off. Apply each additional coat a few inches past the first coat.

What's Next?

We've applied epoxy primer to provide additional adhesion and corrosion protection. Then we applied primer surfacer to fill the minor scratches and small imperfections. Now we're ready to apply guide coat and block sand the primer.

Block Sanding Primer

The car has already been prepped for priming, masked, and sprayed. Now we need to allow the primer surfacer to dry. First let me clear something up so there is no confusion. Some technicians call primer surfacer, primer filler. This is because it is designed to fill small scratches and other imperfections. However, it is the same thing. Another thing to remember about this type of primer is that it must be block sanded.

What You See Is What You Get

Block sanding is performed to level the surface. All lows, scratches, or any other minor imperfections must be completely removed. If you leave a small chip or scratch it will show up in the paint job. In fact, sometimes the glossy clear coat will magnify the imperfection. That is why I say in the title, what you see is what you get. If you can see it in the primer, you will definitely see it in the paint.

Some Steps Cannot Be Rushed

You're almost done, it's primed, now all that you have to do is block it and get it in the booth to paint. It's tempting to rush the drying time, but not allowing the primer surfacer to fully dry is a common mistake made by students. However, this can cause problems for you. Primer may feel dry to the touch, but it may still have solvents evaporating. As solvents evaporate, the primer shrinks.

Therefore if you rush the sanding process, you may have it perfectly sanded. However, after the solvent finishes evaporation the primer shrinks and may actually suck up into the scratches that it was sprayed over. This is called sand scratch swelling. And I have even seen it happen after the car has been painted. To eliminate this be sure to wait the recommended dry time according to the primer p-pages. Every product and paint company is going to be different so read the p-page for the specific primer that you are using.

Is Bigger Better?

This is true in this case. The bigger the block the better results you will get. Use a block that fits the panel contour and use one that is big, but fits the area. You can think of blocking like leveling. If you were going to level the ground, would you want to use a tractor with a narrow blade that covered about 4 ft. or would you use a blade that covered 10 ft? Well, of course you would want to use the biggest one, but if you were only leveling a 4 ft.

wide strip for a sidewalk, the smaller blade would do a better job. The 10 ft. blade may tear someone's yard up. Blocking primer is the same way: bigger is better, but make sure it is a fit for the job. The last thing you want to do is hit an adjacent panel or molding on the vehicle.

Cross Sand

Cross sanding is sanding in one direction, then cross sand going the other direction. This will produce a level surface. You will also want to use long sanding strokes. Little short strokes may make your finished product to look choppy. Back to the tractor leveling the ground. Would you blade little short passes back up and additional short passes, or would you blade with long and even passes across the entire area being leveled. I have never done this kind of work, but I imagine that I would want to use long even passes to level the grade. Therefore, cross sand using long even passes.

Work Smarter, Not Harder

Use tools and methods to help make the job easier for you. One of the methods is to use a guide coat. This is a spray or dry coating that you can apply to the surface that has a contrasting color. This will help you identify the lows, scratches, etc. The goal is to sand all the guide coat off without sanding through to the filler or metal. However, DO NOT use the edge of the block or try to sand the guide coat by hand to remove it. If it is not coming off when blocking, then it is doing its job. It is identifying a problem. Now you can fix the problem.

Remember this is the step that counts. This is where you need to have a flawless repair. Whatever is not taken care of during the blocking process will show up in the finished project. So make sure what you see is that the repair is ready for paint.

Final Sanding

We took a long time to get here, but professional bodywork takes time. This is the one time we can say, if there is no body work needed and the paint on the vehicle is in good condition (we'll talk about what good condition is later), then skip all the other steps and advance to this one. Well, I'm sure that you know that we can't skip every step....remember proper cleaning. It's going to stay with you, I promise. Seriously, many times people just want to know how to sand and paint a car....well here it is.

One Dime Equals Two Nickels

I have mentioned earlier that there are many ways to get from "A" to "B." Many correct ways, but there are always ways you want to avoid too. The secret is knowing what you can get away with and what you can't. The end result is what matters, but never sacrifice quality work for speed. I am going to give you several answers for this topic. I do not want to confuse you though. Just pick which one fits you and go with it. However, a word from experience. If you go to work for a shop, they may have an exact system of how they want things done. Never go in there as a know-it-all. That will be the fastest way to make enemies. Once they see that you will work hard and do things the way they want them done, they may listen to an idea that you have. However, prove your work ethics first, as no one likes someone new trying to prove how much you know....they don't care. All right, off a little. Work ethics is something I focus on with my students. Very important. Back to final sanding.

Wet Sanding

Wet sanding was the preferred method by many and may still be the favored method for some professionals. Wet sanding was the way I was taught and is actually my preferred method. However, with the vacuum systems many shops have, dry sanding systems have became popular, in addition to environmental concerns of where the waste water drains to. It may be required in your state that the water be captured and hauled off by truck to a waste plant. If you took the SP/2 course in module 1, it discusses that. This may be something that you want to check into before determining a method.

Sizing and Folding

This is how I sanded many cars. If you purchase 3M 400-500 grit wet/dry (black) sandpaper, it normally comes in a 9x11 sheet. If you take the sheet and fold it long ways and tear it, it will give you two pieces of sandpaper. Now take the piece and fold it into thirds. This will make you a nice size to sand with. Be certain to fold the creases tight when folding or the paper will move around on you when sanding. Now you're ready to start sanding.

Only Sand One Section At A Time

This is a big tip, which I learned on my own. I used to sand cars with the entire car in my mind the whole time. The job would grow and grow, and grow. The project would become so big in my head; it would actually take me forever to get it sanded. Then I started imagining sections. The hood may be four sections, the fenders would consist of upper and lower and so forth. I would imagine these sections and tell myself that I am not sanding the whole car, I'm just sanding that one small section. Then when I was done with that section, I would move to the next section. Now that was the only section that I was working on. This may sound silly, but it really works. It helps you with a couple of things. First, it breaks the job down into small manageable tasks, rather than one huge overwhelming task. Second, it allows you to thoroughly sand the car without having to go back over it two or three times due to glossy spots. For instance, do not move to the next section until the section you're working on is completely finished. If you don't use this method, you may find yourself sanding a little here and a little there, which leads to the missed areas. Lastly, you know exactly where you are at. If you go to lunch or take a break, you can come back and pick back up exactly where you left off without even thinking about it. So one section at one time.

The Process

Now, I will share with you a few tips and things to avoid when wet sanding. Remember, if paint is going to peel, it's going to start from an edge many times. This is why we need to sand the edges extremely well. It is a common mistake to see a student sand the heck out of the easy-to-get areas and do a fast and sloppy job on the hard-to-get-to areas and edges. It should be the exact opposite. Well, we don't want anything fast and sloppy, but we do need to focus on the edges.

With this in mind, to start, I sand the edges of the section that I'm sanding first. I make sure to get in the crevices, edges, and hard-to-get areas. I also follow up with a scuff pad, but we'll cover that later. When I get my edges sanded, I switch to a new piece of sandpaper so that it is nice and smooth to sand the remaining portion of the section. Once done, I move to the next section and do the same thing. Use my edge piece for edges and my smooth piece for the flat areas. Easy enough, but there are a few things that you want to avoid. Always do the edges first. If you do them last you may leave marks in the paint from the sandpaper. Also, use your hand as a block. Do not use your finders to sand. Use the flat part of your palm creating a block. Sanding with your finger tips may leave marks that show up in the finished paint job. Some professionals use hand pads to eliminate this problem. They work well for the flat areas. One last thing before we move on. When sanding, sand in all directions. You can still use your cross sanding method. However, be sure to make long smooth sanding passes. Short scrubbing style may result in a choppy finish.

Complete

In a nutshell, wet sand the entire car (if complete paint job) with 400-500 grit sandpaper. Break the job into smaller tasks by imaginary sections on each panel. Do not move to the next area, until completely done with the area you are working on. Sand the edges first followed by sanding the remaining part of the section. This exact process is how I sanded many cars. Now you're ready to scuff wash, mask, and paint.

Dry Sanding

I am going to pause in the process for just a minute as the remaining steps are going to be the same. As I mentioned, many shops prefer to dry sand, rather than wet sanding. Similar steps can be used, but a different sandpaper is used. One tip when dry sanding is to have a piece of scuff pad and use it to frequently rub it against your sandpaper to clean the sanding dust off. This will also keep the sandpaper from clogging and scratching the paint surface.

You can also use a dual action sander with a 6 inch sanding pad. When using a dual action sander when final sanding, always use the inter surface pad. Below there is a video demonstrating how to final sand a new OEM part. The same process could be used for a complete paint job if needed. This method is much faster than sanding by hand, but requires more skill to control the dual action sander without scratching or marring the surface. Regarding the sanding method, now we can continue the prepping process.

Scuff Wash

I don't know if scuff washing is a textbook term or not, but it's a system that I developed to assure the vehicle was clean, sanded, and all silicone and other contaminants were removed.

The car has been sanded with 400 to 500 grit sandpaper. Now we're ready to wash it and get it ready to mask. So what scuff washing is, is using a red scuff pad (when painting the entire car) and comet or Ajax, and water. Sprinkle a little Ajax on the wet scuff pad (Scotch-Brite) and scrub the vehicle. This is your chance to scuff all the hard-to-get areas and edges extra well. Be sure to get your edges well, but be very careful not to hit molding, glass, chrome, or adjacent panels that are not going to be refinished. Nothing looks worse than an awesome looking paint job with sanded and scuffed moldings. Now, this is just an extra step that I take, but you can just dry scuff the entire car if you would rather. I just think that the cleanser helps kill any silicone and contaminants. If you do use the water and cleanser, extra time washing and rinsing the car to make certain that all the residue is completely removed is needed.

Wash

Now the car is scuff washed or dry scuffed, back to the soap and water. Thoroughly wash the car. You also need to keep in mind all the dirt in all the crevices that may end up in the finished paint job if not cleaned properly. So start out by washing the jambs in the engine compartment, door jambs, and trunk jambs. Don't forget to wash wheel well areas. Use a different wash mitt and wash bucket when washing jambs. You do not want the dirty and greasy mix that comes from jambs to get smeared into the wash job of the outside of the car. Once all jambs are washed, I normally shut all the doors, hood, trunk lid, then rinse the entire car off really well. If you have a pressure washer, that works even better.

Now wash the outside of the car from top to bottom and rinse or pressure wash well. Now that we washed the car really well, all the residues from the cleanser and/or sanding dust is off the surface and the car is clean. I usually allow the car to air dry at this point. Blowing with compressed air will speed the drying process, if you need to speed up the process.

The Last Step

I normally do one more step before masking. That is to blow the car off with compressed air. I concentrate on panel gaps, wheel opening, molding, or anywhere else that dirt may be hiding. Now we are ready to mask the car and finally get some paint on it.

Masking For Paint

I have already discussed masking for primer. Masking for paint follows the same concept, but there are a few things that differ. Remember when I said to mask to the edge when priming? That is because you do not want primer where it does not need to be. Well, with painting, you want to mask about 1/4" inset into the jambs. For instance, you want a little of the paint overspray to lap over the jambs. If you mask to the edges, you will see a hard edge that is very noticeable.

Jambs First

While I am discussing masking jambs, you also want to do your jambs first. You have to think about it. If you mask the outside of a door first, it may it difficult to open the door without ruining the masking job.

Jamb Masking Techniques

There are several different methods to achieve this. One method is to mask 1/4 inch back from the jamb edge. You can use 3/4 inch tape and 3 inch masking paper. However, straight masking with this method will leave a hard edge from the paint.

Back Masking

This is a reverse mask technique that makes a softer edge. Basically, you simply fold the paper over and allow the tape to be slightly pulled, creating a soft edge. Check out the video and back masking will make sense.

Aperture Tape

This is a foam that makes a seal between the two jamb areas. This method works extremely well and is a fairly simple and quick method.

Transitional Tape

If you want an absolutely invisible repair, then consider using the transitional tape. This tape is amazing. It has adhesive in the middle of the tape, which creates a smooth edge. May or may not be recommended by paint manufacturer, but you can literally apply this tape on a body line and not be able to see the clear coat line. Be sure to watch included videos to grasp the full understanding of these masking techniques.

Do not draw outside of the lines.
Remember in kindergarten the teach had us outline everything in black? They would tell us to keep it in the lines. Well, masking is a similar process. Now that the jambs are masked and the doors are shut, you can start on the outside of the car. First you need to outline everything with 3/4 inch masking tape. So for example, mask around the doors glass, windshield, back glass, or anything else that you are masking off. One piece of advice when outlining your project. It's better to have a little paint on the molding than to have the masking tape of the part being painted. You want a clean job, but it's better to see a trace of paint on a molding than an unpainted chunk on the part. Also, if the paint and clear coat coatings bridge, that is the coatings completely cover the tape and part without a line left behind, you will probably pull a chunk of paint and clear off when unmasking. Besides, you can always clean a little paint off a molding, but a chunk of paint missing is going to require a repaint.

There are some other specialty masking products and techniques that will be covered in videos. Be sure to watch all videos to see the different methods.

Now the car has been properly prepped. In the booth it goes, final masking, and you're ready to start the spraying process.

Module 7 Resources

Visit www.TeachMeHow.info and sign into the members website to access the resources below.

Note: I am providing you with two different lines that I am familiar with. We use PPG and Shop Line at the college. Shop Line is a lower cost line owned by PPG. I am also providing another line of products by Kustom Shop, which I have had good luck with as well. There are many other good brands as well. PPG is what I have used most of my career and am most familiar with. If you have questions about other paint lines, ask in the Q&A and I will try to find the answer for you. Or if you have the answer to any questions, feel free to jump in and help answer. Also note that I only listed one color of primer. The technical data and MSDS will be the same for all colors. I prefer only using one color to keep it simple. However, I use different colors of sealer for hiding, which we will review in the next module.

Audio

1.   •Module 7 Text Podcast
Videos
1.   •Prepping For Primer

2. •Featheredging
3. •Final Sanding Dry DA Sander
4. •Wet Sanding by Hand
5. •Masking For Primer
6. •Foam Tape
7. •Mixing Epoxy Primer
8. •Spraying Epoxy Primer
9. •Spraying Primer Surfacer
10. •Block Sanding Primer
11. •Q&A The Difference Between Primers

PowerPoints
1. •No PowerPoints for this chapter

Product Information

1. •Featheredge Sandpaper
2. •DA Sander
3. •DeVilbiss Spray Gun - Use 1.8 for Priming
4. •Masking Paper 18" Most used width. It comes in may different sizes.
5. •Masking Tape 3/4"
6. •Masking Tape 1 1/2"
7. •Epoxy Primer - Kustom Shop
8. •Epoxy Primer -Shop Line (read technical sheet for info…check local supplier for cost.)
9. •Primer Surfacer - Kustom Shop

10. •Primer Surfacer-Shop Line (read technical sheet for info…check local supplier for cost.)
11. •Guide Coat
12. •Blocks for Dry Sanding
13. •Sandpaper For Blocking - 220 Dry
14. •Sandpaper For Blocking - 320 Dry
15. •Block For Wet Sanding
16. •Sandpaper For Blocking - 220 Wet
17. •Sandpaper For Blocking - 320 Wet
18. •Final Sand - 400 Dry
19. •Final Sand - 400 Wet
20. •Soft Hand Pad
21. •Final Sand 3M Dry System
22. •Interface Pad For Final Sanding

Product Technical Sheet
1. •Kustom Shop DTM Epoxy Primer .pdf
2. •Epoxy Primer Shop Line
3. •Primer Surfacer - Kustom Shop
4. •Primer Surfacer - Shop Line
5. •Guide Coat

MSDS
1. •Epoxy Primer - Kustom Shop
2. •Epoxy Primer Catalyst - Kustom Shop
3. •Epoxy Primer Shop Line
4. •Primer Surfacer - Kustom Shop
5. •Primer Surfacer Catalyst - Kustom Shop

6.   •<u>Primer Surfacer - Shop Line</u>

7.   •<u>Guide Coat</u>

Websites
- No Websites For This Module

Module 7 Training Activity

I know, there is a lot of information in this module. However, this is where it's all at. This is what separates the pros from the non-pros....this is what makes the difference. Read the text content and watch videos. Read all of the technical sheets. Take your panels that you have been practicing on and apply epoxy to the damaged area. Allow to flash and apply two coats of primer surfacer. Allow to dry the recommended time, apply guide coat and block them out.   Additional primer surfacer may need to be applied and re-blocked. Below are the step-by-step memory joggers to help you along the way. Lastly, complete module 7 quiz.

Step-By-Step
Paint Complete Panel That Had Damage Repaired

1.   •The body work is completed and finished out in 150 grit sandpaper.

2.   •Featheredge around the repair area layering each layer of coating at least 1/4" with 220

using a DA - No interface pad needed for this step

3. •Final sand the entire panel (we're painting the entire panel) using a DA sander, interface pad and 500 grit sandpaper.

4. •Scuff the entire fender area with a red scuff pad. Focus on edges and hard-to-get areas.

5. •Blow with compressed air and wipe with wax and grease remover.

6. •Mask adjacent panels to prevent overspray.

7. •May need to cover car with plastic to prevent overspray.

8. •Wipe once again to remove any finger prints and other contaminates.

9. •Mix epoxy primer - check to see if there is an induction time

10. •Apply the recommended number of coats to the damaged area. (corrosion protection)

11. •Mix and apply primer surfacer to damaged area. (filling)

12. •Note: Remember it is only necessary to prime damaged area, not entire fender.

13. •Apply guide coat

14. •Dry block sand with 220 grit sandpaper until guide coat is removed

15. •If low areas or other imperfections still exist, repeat the primer and blocking step.

16.   •If the repair area block out good, switch to 320 grit and block out 220 scratches.

17.   •Using the DA sander with 500 grit and the interface pad, sand the repair area overlapping to the previous sanded area.

18.   •Scuff wash the panel with red scuff pad. Comet (optional)

19.   •Wash with dish soap and water.

20.   •Blow dry

21.   •Mask jambs

22.   •Outline adjacent panels

23.   •Mask using 18" around outline

24.   •Cover car with plastic and tape plastic edge to paper. Note: Do not have plastic too close to the area that you are painting. The dry paint may blow off when the air pressure of the gun hits it. This may result in a big paint flake in your paint job.

25.   •Now you're ready to wipe, tack, and start the spraying process, which we'll cover in the next module.

Tip: You may also want to tape adjacent panels during the sanding process to prevent accidentally hitting the surface, causing scuff marks and scratches. Same goes for molding and chrome.

Steps For Complete Paint Job....No Body Work.

1. •Wash entire car thoroughly with dish soap and water
2. •Wipe with wax and grease remover
3. •Remove all possible parts. Get a baggy for each part and use a sharpie to write the part name on it. Right tail light, right door handle, etc. and put all of the hardware in the labeled baggies. Then put parts in a large container for storage.
4. •Remove any stripes or decals
5. •Mask chrome or molding to prevent scuff marks.
6. •Sand the entire car one section at a time with 500 grit on a DA with interface pad, or with 400 grit wet sanding method using a soft hand pad. Only sand enough to dull surface. A flat surface with no gloss is the goal.
7. •Scuff wash the entire vehicle with red scuff pad, focusing on edges and hard to get areas. (comet is optional)
8. •Wash entire vehicle with dish soap and water. Rinse very well. If comet was used you may want to wash twice to assure all residue is off.
9. •Blow dry with compressed air.
10. •Mask jambs.

11. •Outline glass, moldings, etc. with 3/4" masking tape.

12. •Mask the outlined areas with 18" masking paper.

13. •Now we're ready to wipe, tack, and start spraying.

Steps For Blending Within a Panel

1. •The body work is completed and finished out in 150 grit sandpaper.

2. •Featheredge around the repair area layering each layer of coating at least 1/4" with 220 using a DA - No interface pad needed for this step

3. •Final sand the entire panel (we're clear coating the entire panel) using a DA sander, interface pad and **800** grit sandpaper.

4. •Scuff the entire fender with area with a **gray** scuff pad. Focus on edges and hard-to-get areas.

5. •Blow with compressed air and wipe with wax and grease remover.

6. •Mask adjacent panels to prevent overspray.

7. •May need to cover car with plastic to prevent overspray.

8. •Wipe once again to remove any fingerprints and other contaminates.

9.   •Mix epoxy primer - check to see if there is an induction time

10.   •Apply the recommended number of coats to the damaged area. (corrosion protection)

11.   •Mix and apply primer surfacer to damaged area. (filling)

12.   •Note: Remember it is only necessary to prime damaged area, not entire fender.

13.   •Apply guide coat

14.   •Dry block sand with 220 grit sandpaper until guide coat is removed

15.   •If low areas or other imperfections still exist, repeat the primer and blocking step.

16.   •If the repair area is blocked out well, switch to 320 grit and block out 220 scratches.

17.   •Using the DA sander with 500 grit and the interface pad, sand the repair area overlapping to the previous sanded area.

18.   •Scuff wash the panel with **gray** scuff pad. Comet optional)

19.   •Wash with dish soap and water.

20.   •Blow dry

21.   •Mask jambs

22.   •Outline adjacent panels

23.   •Mask using 18" around outline

24.   •Cover car with plastic and tape plastic edge to paper. Note: Do not have plastic too close to the area that you are painting. The dry

paint may blow off when the air pressure of the gun hits it. This may result in a big paint flake in your paint job.

25.   •Now you're ready to wipe, tack, and start the spraying process, which we'll cover in the next module.

A Blend Panel With No Damage - Blending for color matching only

1.   •Wash entire panel thoroughly with dish soap and water

2.   •Wipe with wax and grease remover

3.   •Remove parts, door handle, etc.

4.   •Remove any stripes or decal

5.   •Mask chrome or molding to prevent scuff marks.

6.   •Sand the panel using 800 grit on a DA with interface pad, or with 800 grit wet sanding method using a soft hand pad. Only sand enough to dull surface. A flat surface with no gloss is the goal.

7.   •Scuff wash the part with gray scuff pad focusing on edges and hard to-get-areas. (comet is optional)

8.   •Wash part with dish soap and water. Rinse very well. If comet was used you may want to wash twice to assure all residue is off

9.   •Blow dry with compressed air.

10. •Mask jambs
11. •Outline glass, moldings, etc. with 3/4" masking tape.
12. •Mask the outlined areas with 18" masking paper.
13. •Now we're ready to wipe, tack, and start spraying.

Additional Resources

I have many additional resources that will be included at the end of this book. However, I do not want to include them under each chapter. As an instructor, I am aware that too much is not always a good thing. Information overload may leave you feeling behind, confused, and/or burned-out. Therefore, concentrate on the information and resources in each chapter. Once you have completed the book, you can explore the additional resources. Again, don't stress about getting through all of the additional resources all at once. Remember simplicity...keep it simple.

Module 7 Preparation Quiz

Once you have completed the module content, take the module 7 quiz below. Please note that you must score 75% or higher to receive a certificate. This quiz has 31 questions. There is not a time limit set on this quiz so take your time. Find the correct answer if you do not know for sure. **The objective of this quiz is to help you learn the information if you do not know the answer, not guessing.** Good luck!

MODULE 8 PAINT

"Spray Gun Adjustments, Maintenance, and Spraying Techniques"

As a painter, your paint job finish (the end result) will depend on your spray gun. This is one piece of equipment that I would make the best buy possible. You also need to treat your spray guns with respect. Keeping them cleaned and well maintained is essential to producing professional paint jobs.

No Lunch Breaks - Clean Immediately

Many of your products consist of two or more parts. For example, primer may have catalyst. Any time the material is catalyzed, it is going to have a shorter pot life. The pot life time and all the other specific information about the product that you're using is listed on the product technical data sheet. The reason that I mention this is because leaving a catalyzed product in your spray gun too long can ruin your gun. Therefore, always look at the technical data sheet and be aware of how long you have to use the product. If you exceed that time, you may have a gun full of a hardened product. That is something that you never want to happen. The pot life can vary from as little as 10 minutes to hours. So don't go to lunch or take a break before cleaning your gun. Always clean it immediately after each use.

How To Clean

There are several different methods for cleaning guns. I have videos demonstrating how to perform each method.

You Made It This Far

One of the common problems that I have seen as an instructor is students trying to paint with a gun that is not spraying correctly. An improperly cleaned paint gun can cause a number of problems, which could have been prevented if the spray gun would have been properly cleaned the prior use. You've spent hours repairing and prepping this car, don't let a dirty spray gun ruin it for you.

Hand Cleaning

Always keep safety first. Wear gloves, eye protection, and a paint respirator to protect yourself from the chemicals. To clean a paint gun by hand, you are going to need cleanup lacquer thinner, a little squirt bottle (like the ketchup and mustard bottles at a restaurant) or a spray bottle, and a gun cleaning kit. First, pour the remaining material out (catalyzed products cannot be saved, as they will harden in the paint container or paint cup) so pour remaining product into your waste container. I have used a five gallon thinner pail for waste storage before. You want to make sure that it has a lid that you can seal it with. You must also contact someone like Safety Clean to dispose of waste. Just like with oil, it's illegal to pour it out on the ground. All right, we have the remaining primer or paint poured into the container, now get your bottle and squirt thinner in the cup, put the paint cup lid on, and swish it around. Pull the trigger (without air pressure) and allow the thinner to stream into the waste container. Repeat this step several times until the stream is clear. Then take the air cap off of the paint gun and brush the gun tip and the air cap. Now use a clean wipe-all with a little thinner on it to wipe the gun inside and out. Next, dry the gun with a clean towel and store it for the next use. If you will do this every time, it will save you time and money in the end, as well as produce awesome quality paint jobs.

Gun washers do basically the same thing, but help you reuse and recycle the thinner. Some systems even have a bake system that recycles your thinner, which may eliminate the need to have your waste hauled.

Spray Guns
There are basically 3 types of spray guns that I am familiar with. They are the siphon feed, gravity feed, and pressure feed. Each gun sprays a little differently and is designed for different types of applications. Well, actually, the siphon feed was

outdated by the gravity feed spray gun. However, they are all designed to do the same thing. They are designed to take the coating being applied and transfer it from the paint cup onto the surface being sprayed. The correct gun setting, fluid needle and nozzle size, and even the quality of the gun can make a big difference of how well the coating looks once applied. (Smooth, rough, orange peel, dry, etc.) Therefore, always read the procedure pages or technical sheets (same thing) to determine what size of fluid nozzle and needle and air cap is recommended for the type of coating that you are going to be spraying. You also need to read the recommended air pressure, how many coats, etc. The quality of the gun can make a difference as well; this is one item that I would not try to go real cheap. Trust me, there are some junk guns out there.

Air Pressure

Air pressure is an important adjustment to setting your gun to spray correctly. Too much air pressure will over atomize your material and too little will not atomize it enough. So what is atomization? Well, that is the process of taking the coating that is the paint cup and breaking it up into smaller parts (drops) and applying it to the surface being sprayed. That is basically what a paint gun is designed to do.

If you could imagine a high gust of wind hitting water, or perhaps pouring a glass of water out going down the road at 90 MPH, how would the water react? It would go everywhere, right? Now, stop the car and pour the water out....it would pour with just a small stream. Well, a spray gun is the same way. We need to find the best setting to have the air break up (atomize) the material to provide a nice, smooth texture to produce a top-notch paint job.

Too much air pressure will cause the drops to be too small and will result in the material going everywhere. This can result in wasted material by causing too much over spray, then when the over spray finally lands on the surface, it will cause a dry film on the top surface that looks dull, dry, or fuzzy. High pressure may also cause your gun pattern to shoot a figure 8 pattern, which can cause stripes and uneven coverage.

Too little air pressure will cause the drops to be too big and result in drops that may not be able to flow into each other. This will cause a heavy orange peel (more depth in paint defects will be covered in module 11) effect.

No Absolutes

As I mentioned, the procedure page will tell you what air pressure is recommended. However, unlike mixing ratios this is not an absolute. There are several factors that may require you to fine-tune your air pressure.

Adjust Air Pressure Where????

One thing that I think is confusing to many people is where to set the pressure. Many procedures state to set the air pressure at the air cap. Well, not too many guns have air gauges on the air cap. If you use the air cap setting from the recommendation and use this psi to set the regulator on the gun, you're going to be spraying very big drops, as the pressure will be too low. Again, if you set the pressure to the recommended setting at the wall, your pressure is going to be too low. So to set it at the air cap, you will need a gauge on the air cap. You need to look for the setting that says at the gun. This means what pressure should be used going into the spray gun. Many painters, including myself, use a regulator at the end of the gun. This allows you to adjust the air pressure at the gun by adjusting the regulator. This is the simplest way in my opinion, but some painters do not like using regulators and prefer to use the wall regulator. If you do that, you will need to consider that for every foot of air hose, there will be a pressure drop. If you set it at 20 psi at the wall, you will not have 20 psi at the gun.

These are a few things to consider when adjusting your air pressure.

Fan Adjustments

This is the adjustment that adjusts your fan pattern. It can adjust it from a small diameter circle to a wide fan pattern. The specific job that you are performing will determine the setting that you use. For example, if you are priming a small area, you want a small pattern to avoid getting primer all over everything. However, if you are painting a complete paint job, you want a wide pattern to cover evenly and fast.

Wide Open

Some painters may prefer to open the fan up as far as it will go, but I have found problems doing that. I am not saying that they are not right, as you will have to find your own technique. Painting is like welding, you need to start off with some recommendations and then fine tune it to your unique style. I find that the fan pattern wide open can cause a dry effect to occur. It is hard to keep the wet edge and provide the gloss that I am wanting. A full open fan pattern may also waste more paint as more material is going to be sprayed on the masking paper and in the air when properly overlapping.

Too Small

A fan pattern that is too small will definitely cause problems as well. If you take the same amount of material and shoot a small 3 inch pattern, you're obviously going to have way too much material. This will result in runs, streaks, and a number of other problems. That is why decreasing your pattern to prime a small area will also require you to decrease your fluid adjustment to prevent this from happening.

Fluid Adjustment

This adjusts the amount of fluid that is sprayed out of the gun. It basically sets your gun trigger to a fixed setting. In other words, it will only allow the trigger to pull back to the adjusted amount. The further back you pull the trigger, the further the fluid needle moves back in the paint gun, which allows more fluid to pass through the fluid tip. This adjustment is going to vary on the job at hand as well. If you're priming a small spot, you probably want a smaller fan pattern and less fluid. Therefore, decrease the fan pattern and decrease the fluid adjustment. The adjust for the fluid is directly behind the needle. Simply screw it in to the right (clockwise) to decrease fluid and screw out to the left (counter clockwise) to increase fluid. Just like a water fountain.

When I am setting a gun to spray a full panel or complete, I back the fluid adjustment back all the way and press the trigger (before paint is in the gun) back all the way. Then I screw the adjustment in until I start to feel it move the trigger. Then I screw the adjustment in an additional two turns. This will give me a good starting point. Then I will fine tune the adjustments in the paint booth.

Fine Tuning

Now we are in the booth and we've opened our fan all the way, the fluid adjustment is open all the way, and we can set the gun to the recommended air pressure, let's say 22 psi at the gun. This can be achieved by pressing the trigger halfway. This will only allow the air to come out. When the regulator reaches 22 psi, you can release the trigger. Now on your masking spray test stand, spray the paint onto the masking paper to see how it looks and feels to you. I normally adjust the fan pattern smaller just a little. Now check your air pressure again, as your fan pattern adjustment will change your air pressure. After it is readjusted, set the fluid adjustment. When you spray, are you getting good coverage? If you are, the gun is probably set correctly. If it's dry or not covering well, increase the fluid. If it's too wet or runs instantly appear, your gun is probably set with too much fluid. Make the adjustments and you're ready to start spraying. Each paint is going to be different, so you will need to learn how to fine-tune the gun to your unique style. It will come with a little practice. Don't try to make your style fit the gun. Adjust the gun to fit your style.

Spraying Techniques

Be A Robot
Painting is all about consistency. If you can do it exactly the same way every time, you'll have it mastered in no time. Like the robots that spray. They have been programmed to do the same thing every time. Nice, even passes with the same speed and distance at all times. The angle is always perpendicular to the panel being sprayed. The first things a new painter needs to work on are speed and distance.

Gun Travel Speed

Gun speed is one of the biggest problems that I have noticed with students. It seems like most students have a tendency to spray the bigger areas at a faster speed, then slow way down on small areas like the fender area behind the front wheel or pillars. However, we need to practice on the exact same speed on all parts of the car.

Too Fast

If you spray too fast, you will have problems with coverage and a dry appearance. If the recommendation asks for two coats, two coats too fast is not going to be adequate. It requires that you build the mil thickness required. This may also result in seeing through the paint. (poor hiding) If your clearcoat does not have enough mil thickness, it may delaminate and peel. So gun speed is a crucial part of painting. I know, you see some painters who paint extremely fast, but there is a reason, which we'll cover next.

Distance

Once you get the speed down, you will need to work on distance. Speed alone or distance alone are not that difficult to master. It's getting the speed and distance going well at the same time....that is the trick. Distance can cause some of the same problems that other gun techniques cause. If the gun is too far away, you're going to have a dry look. This is due to the over spray having too long to dry before it hits the panel. To achieve a wetter spray pattern, you will need to move the gun closer. However, too close and you are going to have runs. If you adjust one technique, you must adjust the other. If you move the gun closer to the panel, you must move faster. If you are further away, as when reaching to the middle of a roof panel for example, you have to slow down. I know, this is not rocket science....it's just common sense. Whatever, this is easier said than done. This is the biggest challenge I have as a teacher when teaching a student to spray. For instance, the student may get closer to the panel, but they forget about speed....guess what happens? That's right, sags or runs.

To become a professional painter is going to take practice and the ability to develop your individual technique. What works for me may not work for you. However, there are a few guidelines to follow to help you along your training path. To start, try to spray 8 to 10 inches away from the panel. This is a textbook recommendation, but it is a starting point. Many seasoned painters shoot closer and move faster, but the closer you are to the panel with the paint gun, the less control that you have. Even a small pause or hesitation will result in a sag or run. By using the 8 to 10 inches rule, you will have control and room for error without ruining the paint job. Once you have this mastered, start working on your technique.

Gun Angle

The factory uses an electrical charge for some of their spraying processes. This works awesome as the charge pulls the paint around corners and in crevices, much like a magnet attracts metal objects. However, we do not have that luxury. Therefore, we must make the gun do it for us. This is another common mistake of not correctly covering edges and corners. For example, on many doors at the belt molding area (top by glass) there is a small flat edge. You must make at least one pass with your gun perpendicular to that area. Just holding completely horizontal or vertical will not work. You must follow the contour of the car. The bottom half of most cars will require you to slightly tilt your gun upwards to get the right gun angle. I know, it sounds like a lot of things to remember at once, but with a little practice, it will become second nature without even thinking about it. It's kind of like driving a car. Remember when you learned how? Every detail was critical and made you nervous. Now I bet you jump in the car and drive to work or school without ever even thinking about what is required of you to properly operate the vehicle. It will come, it just takes practice.

Overlap

This is the amount that each spray pattern overlaps the other. It is a lot like mowing. If you're mowing back and forth at the end of one pass, you turn the mower around and align it to start the next pass. If you try to butt the two edges together, chances are that you will leave grass poking up where you missed it a little. To prevent that we slightly overlap the pass we just mowed to assure that we don't miss any. Same thing with painting. If you don't get the proper overlap, the edges may be light and/or dry and uneven. Proper overlap is different for the specific product that you are spraying, but the technical data sheet will state what it should be. For most of the solvent based products that we use today, a 50% overlap is required to achieve the correct mil thickness and coverage. You also want to remember to start your overlap at the edge of the panels. Half on the panel and half on the paper or air. This may seem like a little waste, but it helps you properly cover all edges with the desired results.

Arching

Arching is caused by locking your wrist and only moving at your elbow. This works much like sticking a thumbnail in a shoe string and using it to draw a circle. You get that arching effect going. If you remember to think like a robot and keep the gun straight and parallel to the panel, you will need to bend your wrist to keep that pattern. You may see what you believe to be painters arching the gun on the end of each pass, but they are actually triggering the trigger to only spray air when the gun is arched out. There are techniques when slight arching or fading the paint gun are needed, such as when blending paint, but this is still kept to a minimum, as too much arching will cause the metallic to lay down differently.

Gun Triggering

We just mentioned triggering, but this is just the process of letting off the trigger halfway. At half throttle, you will still have full air pressure, but no fluid will spray out. Then as you complete pressing the trigger, the fluid will begin to spray again.

Medium Coat or Full Wet Coat...What The Heck Is The Difference?

This is a question that I get often about spray application. The procedure technical data sheet will recommend medium wet-coat at times and full-wet coat other times. We've gone through all the trouble setting up the spray gun, can't we just spray it the same way every time?

Medium Wet
Well, there is a difference, but it's not that big of a deal once you understand the idea. First, let's start with base coat. I've seen a lot of students trying to get base coat to a nice, glossy finish, and heavy mils when applying base coat. However, that is not the purpose of base coat. The required mils are very minimal. Basically, the base coat is the pigment, the color.....that's it! All we want is enough pigment to hide what is underneath it. We call that hiding....we want to achieve hiding. Let's think of it like this: we wrap Christmas and birthday presents to hide what is underneath, right? We can achieve this with a super thin piece of wrapping paper. In this case, one sheet achieves hiding. That is all that we need. There is no need to cut out cardboard pieces to hide the present.....that would not hide it any more than the paper would. Now the cardboard may

protect it better, but that is not the objective. So base coat is a pigment used to hide. Therefore, we do not need to try to apply it extremely heavily. If you are spraying base coat with a wet and shiny look, then you are probably spraying too heavily. Base coat should be dull, at least after a minute or two. To get this result we are going to adjust our gun and travel speed to achieve this. That is why most base coats recommend a medium wet coat.

Full Wet

With a full wet coat we have a different objective. We want the glossy, heavy, and wet look. A full wet coat is almost to the point of sagging or running. Therefore, this can be more difficult to achieve. Let's look at clear coat for example. It's clear so hiding is not the objective. The objective is gloss and protection. Back to the present, if we decided to ship the present, I don't think it would get there without having the thin wrapping paper torn to pieces. So we need something to protect the paper. We mentioned cardboard earlier, but let's get a little more visual. Let's say we cut 1/4 inch plexiglass to fit perfectly around the present. Then we used a strong clear adhesive to glue the ends and edges up. Now you would still see what the wrapping paper looked like and have the protection to keep it from tearing. That is basically what clear coat is used for. So with this thought in mind, a heaver and thicker coat is needed to achieve the required mil thickness and gloss level. There are several ways to achieve this. With clear coat it will recommend a bigger fluid needle and nozzle. This will apply a heavier coat, as the gun is designed to apply heavier coats. However, I have found that I like making a few minor adjustments to the same size gun to apply clear coat. For instance, both increasing your fluid adjustment and narrowing your fan pattern a little will achieve the same result. (full wet) You can also adjust your speed and distance to achieve a full wet coat. One word of caution when spraying full wet coats, well, actually a few things. Do not rush your flash times. You are already spraying the material on thick, so if you rush to your second or third coat too soon, you may create runs or trap solvents from the first coat before they have the opportunity to escape. If this happens, you will have solvent popping which looks like pin holes. This is caused by the solvent evaporating after the material has setup, which leaves a small crater in the paint finish.

Module 8 Resources

Visit www.TeachMeHow.info and sign into the members website to access the resources below.

Audios

1.   •Module 8 Text Podcast

Videos

1.   •Spray Gun Maintenance
2.   •Gun Washer
3.   •Hand Wash Guns
4.   •Paint Guns Q&A
5.   •3M Primer Gun
6.   •Refinish Techniques

PowerPoints

1.   •No PowerPoints for this module

Product Information

1.   •Iwata Paint Gun
2.   •DeVelbiss Paint Gun
3.   •Paint Gun Cleaning Kit

Product Technical Sheet

1.   •No product technical sheets for this module

Websites
- No Website For This Module

Module 8 Training Activity

Read the module 8 text, listen to the audios, and watch the videos. If you have a spray gun, practice with some of the techniques covered in this module. If you do not have any paint material or a place to spray it, practice with water. This will not help you see how the material covers, but you can practice your adjustments, speed, distance, overlap, etc. **After you have practiced the spraying techniques, what do you find is your biggest challenge to overcome as a painter? Post in Q&A Discussion section.** Lastly, complete module 8 quiz.

Step-By-Step
1. •No step-by-step procedures for this module, just keep practicing.

Additional Resources

I have many additional resources that will be included at the end of this book. However, I do not want to include them under each module. As an instructor, I am aware that too much is not always a good thing. Information overload may leave you feeling behind, confused, and/or burned-out. Therefore, concentrate on the information and resources in each module. Once you have completed the book, you can explore the additional resources. Again, don't stress about getting through all of the additional resources all at once. Remember simplicity...keep it simple.

Module 8 Spray Gun Adjustments and Spraying Techniques Quiz

Once you have completed the module content, take the module 8 quiz below. Please note that you must score 75% or higher to receive a certificate. This quiz has 24 questions. There is not a time limit set on this quiz so take your time. Find the correct answer if you do not know for sure. **The objective of this quiz is to help you learn the information if you do not know the answer, not guessing. Good luck!**

MODULE 9 PAINTS AND CLEARS

"Sealers, Base Coat, Tri-Coat, Clear Coat"

This module, I am not going to spend time on the history of paint, as there is not much of it around. The first car I painted was with lacquer and the second was acrylic enamel. It was not long into my career that the industry changed to the base coat/clear coat urethane systems, which are much better and easier to use in my opinion. The industry is currently making another transition to waterborne base coats; however, we're going to stick to the solvents in this module.

Mixing Paint

Before we start painting a car, we must know the paint code. Every car has a paint code from the factory. However, the code may have variations, which may result in additional formulas made by the paint companies. For instance, the paint code may be E9, but there could be several different shades to choose from.

Where Is The Paint Code Located?

That is a good question. Some of them can be difficult to find. I wish all car makers were as simple as Ford, which places them all on the driver's side door or striker area. I think DuPont or one of the paint companies uses the VIN number. With PPG, you must find the OEM paint code. Once you locate it, you can look at the paint book to find the correct PPG number. Then find the various deck with the PPG paint code. A variance deck is all the possible variances for each color. If the particular paint code has four variances, take the cards outside or use a color corrected sun gun to determine which variant is the closest match. Then enter the paint code and variant into the computer and it will provide a paint code for you. Then simply add the amount of each toner that is specified. If you do not have a mixing bank, you will just have to get the paint code and take it to your local auto paint store. If there is a gas lid or another part that you can take with you, that will help them select the best variant. If not, they will usually mix the prime color. That is the first original color.

Don't they use the same color of paint....Why all the variances?

I don't know all the answers to this, but paint can vary from one plant to another. Another thing that I found interesting is that they paint different colors often. I always thought they would paint x amount of cars white, and x amount blue, etc. However, they do not do that. One may be red and the next one white. I don't know this for sure, just a guess is that they paint by demand. I don't know, it seems like that could be streamdlined a little. I know we cannot do like Henry Ford did with the Model A and paint them all black. Well, with this in mind, if you paint a red car, then the system does a clean out rinse cycle, then paint a white car....could you see a potential problem? If there was just a hint of red, it may have a slight tint of red to it. This is not going to be noticeable on the complete car, but when you try to butt match it, you will see that there is a difference. Again, I am no manufacturing expert, just what I have been told and a few guesses. Anyway, for whatever reason, when several painters call PPG complaining about the same color with matching problems, PPG or the paint company will formulate new formulas to match these colors. I know, that is a lot of work, but the good thing is the paint companies do all of that for us; we just need to select the best color and mix the paint.

Single Stage Paint

Single stage is still used today, but most cars from the factory have clear coat applied on them. So unless you are painting a complete, restoring your ride, or cutting costs, you will probably be using the base coat system. Single stage paint is paint that does not require clear coat. It has all the binders and chemicals to provide UV protection mixed into the single stage paint. Now, there is a method of mixing clear with base coat to create a single stage paint to spray your door jambs, engine compartment, and other areas that will not be exposed to the sun. However, if you are painting the outside of the car, you will need to purchase single stage urethane paint that is designed to be sprayed on the outside of the car. I'll add more information about single stage paint in additional resources, but we're going to move on to base coat in this module, as that is probably what you will be working with.

Base Coat

Base coat is the pigment or the color that we see on the car. It is made from three different materials. (1) Pigment, which is the color...may be a dry material. (2) Binders, is the material that binds the pigment and holds it together. It's like a clear glue. (3) Solvents, this is what reduces the material into a liquid form that has the viscosity to spray with a spray gun. That is what makes paint itself. Now there are additional materials added to give different looks and that help dry the paint. Paint may or may not have catalyst, flex additives, or retarders to slow down the dry time. With this in mind, some colors may cover more or less than others. Or certain colors may have more binders and solvents, which causes the color not to cover as well as other colors. Therefore, it is important to understand this as two coats of one color may not be equal to a different color. If the technical data sheet says to spray 2 coats or until hiding, do not spray two coats and call it good. Make sure that it really has full hiding. On the other hand, if it has good hiding, then stop....that is all you need. Remember, the only thing that base coat is for is to cover what is underneath. Do not try to spray base coat wet and glossy...base coat sprays dull, that is what it's supposed to do. If you apply to wet you may trap solvents and cause solvent popping as we discussed in an earlier module or cause metallics to become uneven and cause stripes or mottling in the paint.

Primer Sealer

The main purpose for sealer is to help achieve hiding quicker. For instance, if you have a repair area that has a spot of light gray primer on it and the car is dark maroon, it may take many coats of paint to achieve full hiding. As we mentioned, some colors do not cover well. It would be much better and cheaper to spray one coat of dark sealer over the primer spot, followed by several coats of color. Some painters have even used old paint that has a close shade to the car and use that as a sealer.

Of course, there are other ways to do this. Some primers are designed to be tinted. This will create a primer surfacer that is already a close color to the car being sprayed. Therefore, there is no need for sealer to achieve hiding quicker. However, I am a fan of sealer because it is one last coat of material that helps promote adhesion. It is designed to adhere well to the substrate and the paint adheres well to the sealer. The only time that I recommend not to use sealer is when blending. I will only spray enough sealer to cover the primer spot. The less sealer the better as too much sealer will cause you to make your blend bigger.

Metallics

Metallic is metal or aluminum that is ground into very small pieces. This metal is then added to the paint color to achieve the metallic look. With most metallics, more binder must be used to achieve the desired result. Not enough binder will result in the metallic being covered up and buried in the paint. With added binders, you are going to have less hiding. That is why metallics are always a bigger concern when it comes to full hiding.

Metallics also have other concerns to consider as well. It is very important to use correct gun settings and reducers for color match reasons. First, let's look at air pressure. If your air pressure is way too high, you are going to have a lot of over spray. As the over spray finally settles on the surface, the metallic is going to stand up, which means all the metallic is going to be on top. With most colors, if you see more of the metallic than you do on the adjacent panel, what do you think it is going to look like? It's going to look lighter, right? Because you will see more of the metal color. If your pressure is too low it will cause the metallic to be saturated and become buried in the paint. If you see more color than the metallic, the color is probably going to look darker than the original color. The same is true with reducer. Fast reducer will dry too fast, which will not allow the metallic to settle, causing the color to be lighter. Thinner that is too slow will allow the metallic to settle too much which will result in the color being darker. If this is confusing, don't worry about it. It will all come with time. I just wanted to give you a basic understanding. We'll talk about blending below, which will allow us to make invisible repairs without having to be dead-on with the color match.

Pearls

Pearl or pearlescents, even referred to as mica, is made of very finely ground minerals. Pearls provide some of the shifting colors that change with light and the angles you look at it. Pearls are in many color codes from the factory and a pearl with clear base may be used for the tri-coat in many OEM colors. Custom paint jobs, non-OEM, can also be achieved using pearls. Kustom Shop and House of Kolor are two paint companies that specialize in custom non-OEM colors and products.

Tri-Coat

Tri-coat is a mid-coat that is used to tint the color underneath it. It will not cover the base coat as it is very translucent. In other words, tri-coats are a base clear with a hint of color or pearls in them. Similar to a candy color. It is important to use a test panel to determine what the best match will be. Spray the base coat as you normally would on the spray-out card. Then spray one coat of the mid-coat, mask a strip off of the card and spray another coat, mask a strip, etc. What you will end up with is a small panel with 1, 2, 3, coats of mid-coat. Now clear coat the spray out card. Since mid-coat will never achieve full hiding, it will change the tint of the card with every coat of mid-coat that is applied. So which color matches the car better, base with 1, 2, or 3 coats? Then when you paint the car, you will know how many coats of mid-coat to apply to achieve the desired color.

Clear Coat

Clear coat is just that, a coat that is clear. The purpose of clear is to protect and provide gloss. Therefore, you need to be concerned with the mil thickness. If you do not spray enough clear onto the car, it may become weak and start to peel. Delaminating is a problem that you do not want as all the clear must be taken off to repair and repaint the car if this happens. It may take a while for this to happen, it's not going to happen overnight, but this is something we do not want to happen today or several years from now. Clear protects the paint, provides UV protection, and provides a glossy finish. That is the purpose of clear coat.

Blending

Blending is a process of taking the new paint color and transitioning it into the original paint color. It's much like fading from one color to another without being able to tell the color ever changed. It fools the eye into believing that it's a perfect match, when it may not be. I have a video and blog post below that will better explain the blending process.

Module 9 Resources

Visit www.TeachMeHow.info and sign into the members website to access the resources below.

Note: There are many different brands of paint materials to use. In order to achieve color match you will need to visit your local auto paint store. Be sure to ask for the technical sheets for each product that you use. It may be too confusing for me to list every product below. Therefore, I am only going to list the custom paint line called Kustom Shop to keep it simple. If you have a specific question about PPG or Shopline, just ask in the Q&A section. You may need to seek additional assistance for other brands such as DuPont, Sherwin Williams, etc.

Audios
1.   •Module 9 Text Podcast
Videos
1.   •How To Mix Automotive Paint
2.   •HOW2 Spray Sealer and Base Coat
3.   •HOW2 Blend
4.   •Tri-Coat Paint Job

PowerPoints
1.   •No PowerPoints for this module

Product Information
1.   •Primer Sealer - Needs to be the same shade as base coat.
2.   •Base Coat - Price Varies on Color
3.   •Metallic Colors - Price Varies on Color
4.   •Pearls
5.   •Kandys - Tri-Coat
6.   •Clear Coat
7.   •Blending - Mid Coat Clear

Product Technical Sheet
1.   •Primer Sealer
2.   •Base Coat
3.   •Metallic Colors
4.   •Kandy - Tri-Coat
5.   •Clear Coat
6.   •Blending Clear - Under Mid-Coat Section

MSDS
1.   •Primer Sealer
2.   •Base Coat
3.   •Metallic Colors
4.   •Kandy - Try-Coat
5.   •Clear Coat
6.   •Blending - Mid Coat Clear

Websites
1. •Learning To Blend
2. •The Blending Process
3. •Paint Code Lookup

Module 9 Training Activity

Read the module 9 text, listen to the audios and watch the videos. First practice finding your paint code. I know that you may not have a paint mixing system as demonstrated in one of the videos, but just become familiar with it. I have also included a website that can help you determine the paint code of a car. On this website you can add the year, make and model and it will list the colors for that car. You may consider visiting a body shop and asking if you can see their paint mixing system. If you don't know a body shop owner you may try approaching them to tell them that you are writing a research paper over paints. Most shops like to support education, and would be glad to give you a tour. If you do, be sure to post your results in the Q&A section. I'd be glad to read your findings. Next, if you have the materials and place to spray, continue working on the panels that you have been working on. Try spraying the sealer and paint. Then put a scratch in the paint so you can repair and blend the panel as in the video in this module. **Post your results from the body shop visit in the**

Q&A Discussion section. Lastly, complete module 9 quiz.

Step-By-Step - Seal, Paint, Blend, Clear

1. •The part has been prepped, primed, blocked, final sanded, and masked. Now the spraying process.
2. •Clean the surface to be painted with wax and grease remover.
3. •Tack surface, including surrounding masking paper, with a tack cloth.
4. •Read primer sealer technical data sheet.
5. •Mix primer sealer - If blending within a panel, only seal the repair area to help achieve hiding. Use a shade of sealer that is a close shade to the paint being sprayed.
6. •Adjust paint gun setting.
7. •Spray sealer on the repair area with the recommended number of coats. (usually 1-2 coats)
8. •Allow to dry recommended amount of time.
9. •Read base coat (color) technical data sheet.
10. •Mix base coat - If blending only mix enough to spray the repair area, not the entire panel.
11. •Spray the repair area with paint and allow to flash.

12. •Spray a second that extends past the first coat a few inches.
13. •Repeat painting steps until full hiding is achieved. (2 coats are good sometimes, but not every time.)
14. •Note: the remaining steps are when using PPG paint. Other paint may vary.
15. •Reduce base clear 1:1
16. •Add reduced paint and reduced base clear 1:1
17. •Spray another coat with this new mixture. Extend past your previous painted area 6 to 10 inches. Slightly arc the gun on the end of the paint pass. Be careful to limit this as heavy arching will cause the metallic to land differently, which may cause a halo effect.
18. •Allow paint to flash recommended time.
19. •Read clear coat technical data sheet.
20. •Mix enough clear coat to clear the entire panel the recommended number of coats.
21. •Spray a full-wet coat of clear on the entire panel and allow to flash.
22. •Spray second coat of clear. Most recommendation require 2-3 coats.

Additional Resources

I have many additional resources that will be included at the end of this book. However, I do not want to include them under each module. As an instructor, I am aware that too much is not always a good thing. Information overload may leave you feeling behind, confused, and/or burned-out. Therefore, concentrate on the information and resources in each module. Once you have completed the book, you can explore the additional resources. Again, don't stress about getting through all of the additional resources all at once. Remember simplicity...keep it simple.

Module 9 Spray Gun Adjustments and Spraying Techniques Quiz

Once you have completed the module content, take the module 9 quiz below. Please note that you must score 75% or higher to receive a certificate. This quiz has 18 questions. There is not a time limit set on this quiz so take your time. Find the correct answer if you do not know for sure. **The objective of this quiz is to help you learn the information if you do not know the answer, not guessing.** Good luck!

Module 10 Detailing

"Your Work Is Only As Good As What The Customer Considers Good"

Top quality work and customer service is top priority in my books. However, what is top quality to a customer? We can get caught up in perfecting every detail, then returning the car back to the customer dirty and then expecting praise for all of our hard work. If we think about it, the car probably looks like it did before the accident, at least we try for invisible repairs. So at best, the car is the same as it was before the accident. The customer expects that. They already assume that you're the professional, as they chose your shop to have the repairs performed. Therefore, top quality work may not be enough if you want a happy customer who will be a repeat customer.

For example, let's say that you had to replace a quarter panel. You followed all of the recommendations and performed an excellent job. Now is the customer going to see the corrosion protection, the seamless section that you did, or any of the work put into it? No, probably not; all they see is the finished product. Now, if you don't do a good job or mismatch the paint, that will be obvious. So how do we do a little extra to make the customer notices that we are professionals?

Lesson Learned

I learned this lesson when I worked for a body shop in Tucson, Arizona. I was the guy that we're describing. I worked my hardest to do my absolute best on what I considered to be important.

However, time to clean the vehicle up, I was a slacker. That was not important to me. One day my boss pulled me aside and said, "Donnie, you do good work, but your work is only as good as what the customer considers good." Then he described to me that what a customer sees is the finished product. They may not know how to determine a quality repair, but they sure notice when you return their car cleaner than when they dropped it off.

That is what they see. On the flip side of this, if you leave body filler dust on the seat, a little over spray on the glass, etc., they can sure see that. It does not matter how perfect of a job you did; to the customer, you do crappy work. You know, that has always stuck with me and it's made a difference in my work habits and what I considered to be important to the customer, not only myself. I know many shops have a separate person for washing and detailing. If that is the case, make sure that person knows how important his or her job as a detailer is to the shop.

Making It Shine

All right, I have conveyed the importance of cleaning and/or detailing the vehicle before delivery. Now, let's get started. The first thing that you want to do is to determine the level of cleaning or detailing that you are going to do. If you have a $12,000 job, you can spend quite a bit of time on it. However, if you have a $400 job, you may not spend quite as much time in the clean-up stage. This is the minimum that I would recommend for every job.

- Blow inside with compressed air.
- Wash outside.
- Clean over spray if any. (glass, chrome, etc.)
- Wipe jambs clean.
- Vacuum inside.
- Wipe interior clean.
- Clean glass.

I would perform at least these steps on every single job. Now we will continue the process and go through a complete detail process. Again, you determine the level of work that you think is justified for the job. I am going to give you something to consider when it comes to detailing at the end of this module.

Getting set up

It's best to have a dedicated place for detailing and have all of the things that you need handy. You may want a rack to hang spray bottles on and a cart for your other supplies needed. If you need to keep supplies locked, perhaps a cabinet in the detailing area will work. The idea is to make a system that works. You want a place for everything and everything in its place. This will save hours of hunting cleaners and other supplies needed for the job.

Car Soap

We've been pounding for you to use dish soap to prepare a car for refinish, but we have a different objective in mind now. We do not want to use dish soap, but car soap. Car soap is more gentle than dish soap and aids in the drying process. One piece of advice, you do not want to use soaps with wax. We want to avoid wax at this point. That is, if the car has just been repainted. You do not want to apply wax on freshly painted surfaces, so make sure that the soap is wax and silicone free. One more thing, you must be super careful with fresh paint. Have a separate bucket and wash mitt for washing with dish soap and another bucket and wash mitt for final washing with car soap. Spray the bucket and mitt to clean them before every job that you do. A little dirt trapped into the mitt can cause some nasty scratches and swirls in a new paint job. So ensure everything is clean.

Engine Compartment

Start with the engine compartment. Cover electrical components with rags and apply degreaser on the engine compartment. Allow the degreaser to set a few minutes, then use a long handle brush to scrub any built-up grease or dirt area. If you need to, re-wet the surface with a little degreaser and brush the dirty areas. I would not recommend dipping the brush in the clean water that you have ready to wash the car with. I would have a bucket and brush dedicated for engine compartments, tires and wheels, and floor mats. Once the engine compartment is clean, use a pressure washer, or water hose if you do not have one, and spray the engine compartment clean. Then remove the rags and apply dressing to the engine compartment and close the hood.

Tires, Wheels

Next, while I have the same wash bucket and brush out, I clean the tires, wheels, and floor mats. Then spray wheel bright cleaner on the tires and wheels. Note that if you have aluminum wheels, many cleaners may stain them. If this is the case, you may avoid using tire or wheel cleaners. You will need to scrub them extra well with a brush. If not, go ahead and spray the tires and wheels with cleaner. Spray all four of them, as this will give the cleaner a chance to work. Next, scrub the tires and wheel with a brush. You may have to pull the car forward a little to get the bottom of the tires. Now rinse the tires, wheels, and wheel wells with a pressure washer.

Floor Mats

Depending on if your mats are vinyl or carpet will determine how to clean them. These are usually the dirtiest parts of the car. Using compressed air, blow the loose dirt off. Then spray with all purpose cleaner. If they are vinyl, use a brush to scrub them then rinse. If it is carpet, you can still use the all purpose cleaner and dry brush the mats. Then use a vacuum to finish cleaning. I try to avoid getting carpet floor mats wet, as it can give the vehicle a mildew smell, but I know that some detailers prefer to do it that way.

Blowing and Vacuuming Interior

Blowing the inside of the car out will save time and save on your vacuum filter. First remove any of the bigger trash. However, be careful what you consider trash. If in doubt, place it in a container or bag along with the other belongings that might blow out. Then blow the carpet and interior out. This will remove a majority of the dirt. Next, use all purpose cleaner to spray on any stains. Use a brush and dry scrub the stain. Then vacuum the carpet and interior.

Cleaning Interior

Now you can clean all of the interior parts. Dash, plastic parts, etc. Use a rag with soap water and wring it out so that it is not saturated and wipe the parts to remove the excess of the dirt off. Next, using the all purpose cleaner you can spray some on a rag and continue cleaning the interior. A small short bristle brush can work well for cleaning the crevices. Now, you can use some dressing to give it the full luster look. Be certain to always spray the dressing on the rag and not the interior to prevent the dressing getting on unwanted areas. If the dressing gets on gauges, electrical components, glass, and painted surfaces, it can be a mess. While dressing works great for plastics and rubber, it may smear and make a mess on other parts. Another consideration for auto body shops is silicone. 3M and many other companies make silicone free dressing. I would recommend selecting one of these types of dressing unless your detailing area is located in a separate building.

Trunk Area

If you have a truck area on the vehicle blow it out
with compressed air, apply all purpose cleaner to
any stains and dry brush. Then follow up with
vacuuming.

Wash Outside

Now get your clean bucket, car soap and mitt. Add
about 1-2 ounces of car soap to the bucket and add
water. Before washing rinse the car, trying to get as
much of the dirt off as possible. The more you
rinse off the less chance you have of rubbing the
dirt with your mitt, causing swirl marks. Once
rinsed start washing the car with the mitt. Start
from the top and work down. Be sure to keep the
mitt wet by dipping in the bucket. This will help
remove any dirt that may have been trapped in the
mitt. Also note that you do not want any of the
soap to dry on the car. If it starts to dry, re-spray
then continue. Once you have washed the whole
car rinse thoroughly. There may be bugs and other
deposits that require special attention. For bug
spots use a bug brick to remove the spot. If you
feel a texture or rough or dry feel on the glass or
paint, it may be necessary to use a clay bar to
remove and smooth the surface. You want the
surface to feel smooth. Some painters have used
0000 steel wool or razor blades on the glass to

remove over spray, but care must be taken not to scratch the glass. Once everything is spotless, rinse the vehicle again. Now you can dry the car starting from the top and working down.

Dry Jambs
Now that you finished washing the car, open doors, hood, and truck lid and wipe the jambs clean. Be sure to wipe all the rubber seals and plastic pieces too.

Dressing
Now you can use the dressing to spray the tires. I usually just spray the engine compartment and the tires and leave it without wiping the areas with a towel. Again, you may need to pull the car forward to fully cover the bottom of the tires.

Wax
Again, I do not recommend using wax on a new paint job. However, this is where you would wax the car if you're just detailing a car for a customer. If it has just been painted you can use a hand glaze or final detail product, as they do not contain silicone. Silicone seals and protects the paint, but we want to allow the paint to breathe and allow it to fully cure, which make take 30 days. To apply

the wax, simply follow the directions on the can or bottle.

Glaze

Glaze can be applied to new paint. This is similar to wax, but does not contain silicone and does not seal the paint like wax. Glaze gives the paint the full luster to the paint, but does not protect the paint like wax. This can be used after painting a car or after buffing and polishing a new paint finish. This is a hand application. I use one wipe-all cloth to apply the glaze to a panel, then wipe the panel with a dry wipe-all. I do one panel at a time. Once the complete car is done, I normally go over the entire surface being glazed with another dry wipe-all to remove all smudges. Do not be scared to waste wipe-alls. If it becomes dirty, throw it away and get a new one. The last thing that you want is to rub dirt around on the new finish creating scratches.

Clean Glass

I always like to leave the glass for last. This way the glass will have a streak free appearance. This is what the customer looks through, so if they can see spots and streaks, then the job looks less professional.

Now the car is washed, dried, the interior has been cleaned, vacuumed, dressing applied, and now we're ready to prepare the car for delivery for the customer. Now what the customer will see is a nice clean car that looks better than it did before the accident. They may not be able to see all of the work underneath the surface, but they will thank you for what they can.

This Can Be Win/Win If You Do It Right

As I started this with, you may not want to do a full detail on every job. It's up to you how much you want to do. In fact, you may be able to sell them on a full detail when you start repairs. This way the customer will get the nice clean job and you will get an additional fee for the work performed. Think about it....the customer already selected your shop to perform the repairs.... and many people pay for this service anyway, chances are they will pay an extra $100 - $125 (or whatever your rates are) out of pocket to have it all taken care of while it's in the shop.

Buffing and Polishing

This is something that you will probably only do to cars that have been painted to remove small imperfections. Small runs, sags, orange peel, dirt, dry, etc. These are all reasons that you may need to buff. I often hear the term cut and polish, as you are leveling the surface and polishing it back to the full luster and shine. In fact, the finish looks much smoother, slicker, and deeper after a cut and polish. You've seen the cars that look like glass haven't you? Show cars usually have a full cut and polish job. However, depending on the shop policy, you may or may not buff every car that goes through the shop. Most shops only polish the areas that need it. For instance, if there is only one small piece of dirt, many painter will nib that one spot and buff it out. Hopefully, through all of the cleaning steps and maintaining a clean paint booth, you will not have too much dirt. Although, every painter has small imperfections from time to time that need to be buffed out.

There are many ways to sand the surface. This process may be referred to as color sanding. I prefer the method that 3M has. This system uses a dual action sander and fine sandpaper, which we will cover shortly. The other way to sand the surface is with a wet sanding method. This method uses a sanding block and fine grit sandpaper. Nibbing block, razor blades and other tools may be used to level the surface as well.

Leveling

The objective is to sand the imperfection and level the surface. Remember that coarser grit levels and finer grit smoothes and polishes. Also remember to level, you must use a block or the hard surface of a dual action sander. If you use your hand or a soft interface pad when sanding, you will not level the sag or imperfection. You will just end up following the pattern until you have sanded completely through the coating, while the sag is still there. So use a hard surface to level. Once leveled, we can use a soft hand pad or an interface pad with a finer grit sandpaper to polish the surface. Now we'll discuss a few ways to perform these two steps.

3M System

As I mentioned this is my preferred method, but there are many other technicians who prefer wet sanding. Just give them both a try and see which method works best for you. To start, use the DA sander with 6" with 1200 grit sandpaper; lightly sand just enough to level the sag or dirt. Once leveled, use the interface pad and continue sanding the surface. Be careful not to sand on body lines or edges as it will sand through the coating, which may cause repainting. Next, switch 1500 grit to minimize the 1200 grit scratches. Lastly, use 3000 grit sandpaper using the interface pad. This step requires a little water, but not too much. Too much water will not allow the sandpaper to polish properly. Use a squirt bottle to add a few sprays to the surface and begin sanding. Just a few passes in one direction and a pass or two in the opposite direction is usually enough. You want to ensure that the surface builds a white paste liquid. This means that the clear is sanding properly. Clean the surface off and you're ready to buff. We'll cover the 3M system after we cover wet sanding.

Wet Sanding

This was the system used for many years until 3M developed the DA sanding system. To begin, I have found that soaking the sandpaper in water for several hours before using it works best. Using clean water and a mitt or a spray bottle and 1200 grit on a rubber sanding block, sand the imperfection until level. Use the same precautions as above for edges and body lines. One way to prevent sanding through is to tape your edges off with masking tape. Once the surface is level, use a soft hand pad and 1500 grit sandpaper to prepare the surface for buffing.

Razor Blade

There is a much faster way to help level the majority of the imperfection. Works real well on runs and sags. This is by using a razor blade to gently scrape the sag. You must be extremely careful not to allow the edge of the razor blade to dig in and scratch the surface. I've added a video demonstrating this technique. I have had a lot of luck using a razor blade.

Nib Block

They also make a tool for this, which have blades on it to scrape much like the razor blade method. I'm sure that this works well for some painters, but I have not ever had much success with this tool. 3M has a new de-nib tool that looks like it would work well, but I have not had a chance to use it myself so I am not sure how it works yet.

Buffing

I call it the 3M 3 step system because there is a bottle 1, 2, and 3. They are also color coded to make it easy to remember which product should be used with which buffing pad. Step 1 is your compound and use a white foam or wool pad. Step 2 uses a black foam pad, and Step 3 uses the blue foam pad. Step 3 is not necessary to use on lighter colors. It is only used when buffing dark colors. It's an extra step to eliminate swirl marks.

All three steps follow the same basic steps. Apply the product to the surface and rub it in with the buffing pad to eliminate slinging polish everywhere. Then using medium to heavy pressure buff in one direction several passes, then several passes in the opposite direction. Then with very light pressure buff several passes in each direction. It is important to use the medium pressure followed by light pressure. You also want to use a lower RPM than when grinding. 1000 to 1400 tends to work well. There is not an exact science or number of passes it will take, it will just take a little practice and you will develop the technique to perfect the buffing technique. That covers buffing in a nutshell. However, there are other details that will be covered in the resources below. Be sure to watch all the videos and listen to the audios for more details on buffing.

Caution

Caution with sanding or buffing. Stay away from body lines and edges. It is very easy to sand or burn through on these areas. Take extreme care when sanding or buffing in these areas.

After you're done buffing you will need to wash and clean the car as described above. Special attention needs to be taken on gaps and other places that the compounds and polishes may have gotten during the buffing process. You do not want an awesome looking paint job with white compound showing in all the gaps and edges. One thing that you can do to prevent this is to tape the panel gaps during the buffing process. After washing, you can give it the final touch by using a hand glaze over the painted surface to give it the full deep luster.

Module 10 Resources

Visit www.TeachMeHow.info and sign into the members website to access the resources below.

Audio
• Module 10 Text Podcast

Videos
1. •Removing Swirl Marks
2. •How To Sand And Buff Using 3M Products
3. •Color Sanding
4. •3M New Denibbing System

PowerPoints
1. •No PowerPoints for this module yet

Product Information
1. •All Purpose Cleaner

2. •Car Soap - For Detailing....Not For Paint Prep
3. •Claybar
4. •DeWalt Buffer
5. •Super Degreaser
6. •Silicone Free Dressing
7. •Wheel Bright
8. •3M Polish #1
9. •3M Polish #2

10.   •3M Polish #3
11.   •3M New Denibing System

Product Technical Sheet
1.   •All Purpose Cleaner
2.   •Car Soap
3.   •Clay Bar
4.   •Super Degreaser
5.   •Silicone Free Dressing
6.   •Wheel Bright
7.   •3M Polish #1 - Compound - White Pad - Not Available
8.   •3M Polish #2 - Polish - Black Pad - Not Available
9.   •3M Polish #3 - Fine Polish - Blue Pad - For Dark Colors - Not Available
10.   •3M New Denibbing System

MSDS
1.   •All Purpose Cleaner
2.   •Car Soap
3.   •Clay Bar
4.   •Super Degreaser
5.   •Silicone Free Dressing
6.   •Wheel Bright
7.   •3M Polish #1
8.   •3M Polish #2

9.　•<u>3M Polish #3</u>

Module 10 Training Activity
Read module 10 text, watch videos, listen to audios, read the technical data sheets and put it all to work. Detail your own car like this and offer to do a few other family members'. **Share your detailing experience or tips on the Q&A section**. Lastly, complete module 10 quiz.

Step-By-Step
Detail
1. • Raise hood and cover electrical components with rags.
2. • Spray engine compartment with degreaser and allow to soak several minutes.
3. • Scrub dirty areas with brush.
4. • Reapply degreaser to any dry or dirty areas.
5. • Pressure wash the engine compartment and under hood.
6. • Apply dressing to the entire engine compartment and shut hood.
7. • Spray wheel bright on all four tires and wheels. Be careful on some aluminum wheels. If in doubt, just scrub with a brush.
8. • Scrub tires and wheels with brush.

9. • Pressure wash tires, wheels, and wheel wells.

10. • Take floor mats out and blow with compressed air.

11. • Spray with all purpose cleaner.

12. • Carpet matts vacuum - Vinyl matts pressure wash.

13. • Blow inside and interior of car.

14. • Vacuum inside of car.

15. • Clean inside of car with all purpose cleaner.

16. • Spray dressing (ON RAG) and apply to plastics.

17. • Clean and vacuum trunk area.

18. • Pressure wash outside of car.

19. • Wash outside of car from top to bottom. Rinse, wash, rinse. Never allow the soap to dry on its own.

20. • Use clay bar to smooth any rough surfaces on paint.

21. • Use 000 or 0000 steel wool on glass if there is over spray.

22. • Rinse car.

23. • Dry car.

24. • Dry jambs.

25. • Wax or glaze paint surface.

26. • Clean inside and out of glass.

If buffing is needed

1. • Scrape off nib defect. (run, dirt, etc.)
2. • Sand with 1200 on block or DA.
3. • Sand with 1500 on block or DA w/interface pad.
4. • Sand with 3000 on block or DA w/interface pad.
5. • Buff with #1 compound and white pad.
6. • Buff with #2 polish and black pad.
7. • If dark color, buff with #3 and blue pad.
8. • Detail car as described in steps above.
9. • Apply hand glaze.

Detailing is a lot of work, but can make the car look excellent.

Additional Resources

I have many additional resources that will be included at the end of this book. However, I do not want to include them under each module. As an instructor, I am aware that too much is not always a good thing. Information overload may leave you feeling behind, confused, and/or burned-out. Therefore, concentrate on the information and resources in each module. Once you have completed the book, you can explore the additional resources. Again, don't stress about getting through all of the additional resources all at once. Remember simplicity...keep it simple.

Module 10 Detailing Quiz

Once you have completed the module content, take the module 10 quiz below. Please note that you must score 75% or higher to receive a certificate. This is a short quiz with only 10 questions. There is not a time limit set on this quiz so take your time. Find the correct answer if you do not know for sure. **The objective of this quiz is to help you learn the information if you do not know the answer, not guessing**. Good luck!

Module 11 Paint Defects

"Paint Defects and Other Considerations"

We've covered repairing damage, priming, and painting. However, the paint finish is not always ready to sand and shoot. There are many paint defects that may cause you to strip or partial strip the coating before refinishing. There are other paint defects that can occur during the paint and refinish process. This module is going to cover some of the defects and what to do about them.

The first thing that you want to do before ever starting any paint job is to properly clean the service. This step is often overlooked, but leads to many of the problems caused in the refinish and painting process. This may result in adhesion problems, dirt in paint job, and fisheyes. I like to use dish soap as it cuts the greases and silicones off the surface. Many car soaps are designed to wash the car without stripping the waxes.

Examine the paint surface to determine which method to use to prepare the surface for paint. If the paint is peeling, cracking, or too thick, you may need to strip some or all of the paint off of the surface. If the paint is in good condition, you will probably be safe final sanding the surface and re-spraying.

Let's examine the list of reasons that you may have that will require you to strip or partial strip the paint surface. Peeling, micro-checking or cracking, bubbling, and too thick. Then we will talk about blocking and final sanding.

Peeling

This is where the topcoat is peeling off the undercoating. This is due to a loss of adhesion. Painting over a surface in this condition may result in the new paint job peeling as well. The new paint job is only as good as the surface that it is applied to. Just like a building, the foundation is the most important part of the construction. There are different ways to strip the paint of the surface including chemicals, sanding, and media blasting. I prefer to just use a DA and sand the surface with 36-80 grit. You will need to sand down past the surface that was peeling or strip to metal if needed.

If it's the clearcoat, make sure that all clearcoat is off of the panels that are peeling. If the top coating is peeling all the way down to the primer, make sure to sand all color down to the primer on the panel. This will ensure that there will not be adhesion failure at a later time.

Note: If you are restoring a vehicle, stripping a complete vehicle, or have rust, you may consider media blasting. Chemical stripping can be effective too, but new legal concerns are being addressed about the proper disposal of the waste.

Tip: Sometimes you may be able to use a razor blade to scrape much of the paint off. Other methods include using high pressure washer and/or compressed air. These two methods do not work every time, but can save a lot of time if they work.

Once you have the panel stripped with 36 then 80, I like to go over the surface with 150 to 180 grit on a

DA sander to smooth the 80 grit scratches. Once sanded, re-clean the surface with wax and grease remover and prepare for primer. You may check with the paint manufacturer to determine if you need to apply a metal cleaner and/or conditioner. I use epoxy primer (1-2 coats) as a base primer as it offers excellent adhesion and corrosion protection.

Then I use urethane primer surfacer (2 coats), which will give me a nice surface to final sand and prepare for paint.

Tip: It is very important to allow each coat of primer to flash between coats. Read the Technical Data Sheets for the product that you are spraying. Hosing on too thick or too many coats without allowing it to dry will result in a number of different problems. Be sure to allow each coat to flash (dry) the recommended amount before applying the next coat. Also take the temperature into account. The colder the temp, the longer flash required.

Now we have the panel primed and it is ready to prep for paint. We're assuming there is no damage as we are only discussing the paint procedures, but I always use guide coat before blocking or final sanding primer. This is a paint, usually black, that will contrast with the primer. This will help you identify highs and lows when sanding. If there is a low, the black coating will stay in the low area letting you know that your attention is needed to observe the imperfection.

Final sand the surface with 400 to 500 grit sandpaper. You can do this by hand with a block. However, I like to use a DA sander with a 3M interface soft pad to sand the surface. The objective is to sand all of the guide coat off without sanding through the primer coatings.

If low areas are found you will need to determine if the low area needs to be pulled and repaired or if a little glazing putty can be used.

Once you have the panel final sanded, you are ready to wash the panel again with soap and water, then wipe the surface with wax and grease remover.

Mask if needed, as we described in the prep section.

Tack the surface with a tack cloth to remove all fine dust, dirt, and lint.

Mix and apply sealer primer. Sealer promotes adhesion and helps achieve hiding. This will result in using less paint. The sealer should be the same shade as the color of the paint on the car being sprayed. For example, if the car is white, a light or white sealer should be applied. Usually 1 or 2 coats are all that is needed.

Wait the flash time and examine the surface. If you find any dirt, hair, or anything else in the sealer, use 600 grit sandpaper with wax and grease remover to help lubricate the sealer. Gently sand the surface smooth. If you sand through, apply more sealer to the spot. Wipe the area with wax and grease remover and tack the entire surface.

Tip: You can tack between each coat until you get to the clear coat application. Once you start clear coating, be sure to NOT touch the surface again.

Base Coat

Mix and apply base coat. This is the pigment or color. The objective to applying base coat is to apply an even coat to achieve hiding.....not to have a glossy finish. Applying the base coat on too thick can lead to many problems. Problems include: not drying properly, metallic mottling, lifting, and many other problems.

Clear Coat

Mix and apply clearcoat. This is where most of your mils will come from and you want full gloss when you have completed this step. Check your manufacturer's technical data sheet to see how many coats to apply, but usually 2 to 3 coats are sufficient.

Micro-Checking

This is tiny cracks in the paint. These cracks may be easy to see, or checking may be difficult to identify as well. You may need a magnifying glass to get a closer look at the surface. I have found that when a surface has this type of damage it is best to strip down all of the way to the metal. The tiny cracks are deep many times and will cause you problems if painted over. I have heard of technicians sanding the surface down and using a fill primer to fill the small cracks, but I certainly would not recommend that. I recommend stripping down to bare metal and following the procedure as described in the peeling lesson for the refinish process. Epoxy, Primer Surfacer, Final Sand, Sealer, and Paint.

Too Thick

Using a mil gauge you can determine how much paint has been applied to the surface. If the coatings exceed 12 to 14 mils, it is recommended to strip or partial strip the surface. Just like a roof on a house, you can only put one or two layers of shingles on without having to remove them and start over. Usually the OEM paint or factory paint and one additional paint job, you will usually be close to the 12 mils range. So it is safe to assume that if the vehicle has ever been repainted you are getting close to the exceeded limit. Probably 3 paint jobs is a definite sign that stripping will be required. However, stripping to the metal may not be required. Remove enough of the coating to 6 or 8 mils or less. A mil gauge will need to be used periodically to know when you have reach the required mil thickness. This will allow the new coating to be applied within the mil thickness recommendations and still leave the factory undercoatings. To use this method start DA sanding out with 180 grit followed by 220, 320, and final sand with 500 grit. It is also a good idea to use an interface pad for this sanding method. Once final sanded, wash, mask, wax and grease remover, tack off, primer sealer, paint, and clear coat.

Chipping

Chipping may be due to the top coat not having proper adhesion, the mil thickness not being thick enough, or it may just be due to gravel. Even an OEM paint job from the factory will chip if hit by gravel at high speeds. The best way to repair chips is to featheredge them out. If the chip is into the primer, you will need to feather down to the primer. If the chip is into the metal, feather down to the metal. Once chips are feathered out, final sand with 500 and primer small metal areas with self etching primer. Then you're ready to continue with the painting steps. There is another method that I have seen many times. If the chip is not down to the metal, sand with 180, fill with glaze putty (with razor blade) and block out. This is quicker than featheredging; however, if the chip is down to metal, featheredging is required to ensure that all rust traces are sanded and properly treated.

We have reviewed some of the reasons that will require additional steps before painting. Now we are going to review some of the problems that can go wrong during the painting process.

Dirt

I'm sure with all of the cleaning procedures that I have mentioned, that dirt is your enemy in the painting world. This is dirt that can come from your paint booth, the car, or even yourself. We've emphasized to get the car clean, but you also need to make sure the booth is clean. If you do not have a downdraft booth, you may need to wet the floor to keep the dust down. Make sure your hoses are

clean. You must also think of yourself. Are your
clothes clean or do they have lint on them? You
also want to have your arms covered, as you don't
want hair in the paint job, which has happened
many times. Even following all of the cleaning
steps cannot promise a dirt free job. If there is dirt
during the sealing or base coat stages, allow to dry,
lightly sand area with 600 grit to remove dirt,
reapply coat to the sanded area, and continue the
process. However, if dirt is noticed during the clear
coating application, you must complete the clear
coat application and cut and polish after the clear
coat is dry.

Orange Peel
This is a easy term to remember, because it is
actually referring to the peel of an orange. The peel
of an orange has a bumpy texture. Now if you look
close at all paint jobs, even new from the factory,
there is orange peel present. The only time there is
not, is if the surface has been cut and polished
(buffed) like a show car. However, it is the
excessive orange peel that becomes the problem
and becomes an undesirable finish to the customer.

When we were discussing spraying techniques and
how the spray gun atomizes paint, we said the paint
is broken into tiny drops so that it could be
transferred from the cup to the car. When the
drops are too big or too dry when they hit the panel
being finished, the drops will not flow together and
level out as they should. In order to reduce the
orange peel to an acceptable amount, find a way to

make the paint drops smaller or a way to spray the paint wetter.

Before we suggest ways to fix the problem, let's look at a few of the things that could cause excessive orange peel. The more air pressure, the more atomization (smaller drops) and the less air pressure, the less atomization (bigger drops). Therefore, the problem could be that your air pressure is too low. Next, the closer to the panel the wetter the paint is going to be, the further away, the paint has more time to dry before landing on the panel being painted, resulting in dry spray. Therefore, another correction could be to get closer to the panel being sprayed. What else could cause the drops to dry too fast? Using a reducer that is too fast for the temperature that you are spraying could cause this as well. Never try to use a faster reducer thinking that you are going to speed up the process as it can lead to problems such as this. So make certain your air pressure is correct, work on spraying at the correct distance, and always mix the recommended products and you will reduce the chances of orange peel.

Runs and Sags

I have always heard that a run is a painter's signature. It probably will not work for the customer though. Runs and sags are basically the buildup of product, which causes it to run, or almost run, which would be a sag. I am pretty certain that there is not a painter out there who has never gotten a run. I know I have had some and it can really make a good day bad really fast.

However, if the runs are not too bad you can usually repair them by sanding and polishing the area as described in the detailing module. So what causes runs? The obvious is spraying too close, too heavy, or going too slow. Another thing that you may need to think about is flash times. Did you wait the recommended flash time between coats? This is something else that can lead to runs or sags.

To eliminate runs work on gun speed, distance, and always follow the recommendations from the product technical sheet and always use the correct reducer for the temperature.

Sand Scratch Swelling
This is a condition which you can see the scratches in the bodywork. This is caused by using too coarse of sandpaper when finishing your body work, not properly priming and block sanding the repair area, or applying too much primer and not allowing it to properly dry. The first two reasons explain themselves, but let's look at the third reason. It's called hosing it on. Don't try to put extra thick coats on, thinking that it's going to fill more, or rush the coats by not allowing flash times. This can lead to solvents being trapped in the primer. If you rush through a job, primer it, block, seal, paint, clear, all in a short period of time, you are trapping a lot of solvents in the material. It may look great when you are done painting, but when the solvents start evaporating, the coatings shrink,

which leave the scratches with inadequate primer to fill them.

To eliminate this problem, always make sure that your body work is ready for primer. Have filler and surrounding areas sanded with 150 grit to eliminate all of the 36 and/or 80 grit scratches. Apply the coatings as recommended. If it recommends two medium wet coats then apply two medium wet coats....not four double-wet coats back to back with no flash time. More is NOT better in this situation.

Lifting

This is a chemical reaction of the solvents softening the substrate coatings and causing them to lift. Years ago I used a paint called ACME that would lift very easily during base coat application. The cause of this was rushing the flash times or applying the base coat too thick. Once it lifts, it may require stripping to metal. Strong solvents like thinner on fresh paints also cause lifting. You should be extremely careful if you sand through the surface on fresh clear. For example, let's say that you found an additional dent that needs to be repaired and repainted. The ring where the clear coat and base coat sanding through is very sensitive and may lift if re-sprayed. Using a sealer and spraying a light dry coat can help seal the surface and eliminate the lifting problem. So never spray wet with your first coats if lifting is a problem. You must also watch etch primer if you use that type of primer. If sprayed too wet, it may attach and lift the edges.

Therefore, always spray etch primers in thin coats that are not wet.

To eliminate this problem, wait recommended flash times and always use the correct reducers. If you are working with fresh paint, use thin dry coats.

Striping

This is streaks or stripes that can been seen in metallic paint jobs. This is due to the metallic laying uneven due to improper gun settings or spraying techniques. For example, if the air pressure is too high, it will cause a figure 8 (heavy on top and bottom), which will result in stripes. Another reason that causes this is by spraying base coat too wet. This allows the metallics to gather together, which will cause the stripes.

To eliminate this problem, always maintain your spray gun and assure that it's spraying correctly. Spray base coat with a medium-wet coat to ensure that it's not sprayed too wet. Use correct overlap, recommended reducers, and air pressure.

Mottling

This is a blotchy look caused from the metallics gathering together in spots rather than stripes. Again, this can be caused by applying metallic paints too wet, applying clear coat without proper base coat flash time. The clear can actually move the metallic around causing this problem. So the base may have been sprayed correctly, but cause the mottling during the clear coat process. So always allow proper flash time between base coat and clear coat.

To eliminate this problem, always maintain your spray gun and ensure that it's spraying correctly. Spray base coat with a medium-wet coat to ensure that it's not sprayed too wet. Use correct overlap and recommended reducers. And allow recommended flash times.

Solvent Popping

This is small holes or craters that appear in the surface. This is caused from solvent that was trapped in the coatings. As it finally evaporates, it left the void, or hole in its place. As with many of the paint defects, applying too much material too fast is the leading cause for this problem. It could also be due to the bake system, if it was set too hot.

To eliminate this problem, follow recommended film thickness and wait recommended flash time. Avoid overheating the surface during the bake time.

Fish Eyes

This is round circle-looking spots on the surface. This is where the coating will not cover due to silicones. Have you ever spilt oil on the ground and cleaned it? Once clean, you sprayed it with water? Did you notice how the water beads up? Other examples of water beading up are: water in a frying pan, or on a freshly waxed car. With that in mind, let's say that we wax a small circle the size of a dime on the hood of a car. If we run water over the car, the dime-sized spot will immediately dry as the water beads up around it. That is similar to what happens when getting fish eyes in a paint finish. The silicone will not allow the paint to stick in the small dots due to the silicone.

Silicone is in many car care products such as wax, dressings, Armor All, oil, and even in the environment from diesels and many other resources. The vehicle is going to have silicone contaminates when entering the shop. That is why it is important to make certain the surface is properly washed and cleaned. Proper cleaning will eliminate this problem. I have not had many problems with this, but it has appeared, even after cleaning the car. What I was able to do was to spray a light dry coat to seal the surface and wait additional flash time to allow it to dry well. Then I continued spraying in a normal manner. Of course, if the fish eyes are too big or too many, this trick may not work.

To eliminate this problem, clean, clean, clean.

There are other problems that can arise, but this covers the most problems that you will have or that I have had. There are other problems that we may address later, but if you follow the cleaning steps as you have been instructed to do, you should not have many of the problems. In the website resources below, I have added a website that shows some excellent photos and explanations of these and many other defects.

Module 11 Resources

Visit www.TeachMeHow.info and sign into the members website to access the resources below.

Audio
1. • Module 11 Text Podcast

Videos
1. •Stripping Paint To Metal
2. •Scraping Runs With Razor Blades

PowerPoints
• No PowerPoints for this module

Product Information
1. •3M DeNib System
2. •Paint Stripper
3. •Paint Thickness Gauge
4. •Nib Tool
5. •Razor Blades

Product Technical Sheet
1. •3M DeNib System
2. •Paint Stripper

MSDS
1. •Paint Stripper
Websites

1. •<u>Paint Defects</u> - Photos of paint defects by BASF.

Module 11 Training Activity

Read module 11 text and take a look at the different photos of paint defects provided by BASF. **Have you ever seen one of the problems mentioned in this module? Tell us a little about it. Post in the Q&A section.** Complete Unit 11 Quiz.

Step-By-Step

Strip To Metal

1. • Wash panel with soap and water
2. • Wipe with wax and grease remover
3. • Remove coating, DA with 36 followed by 80 grit, or use chemical striper, or media blast
4. • DA sand with 180 grit
5. • Apply 1-2 coats of epoxy
6. • Apply 2 coats of primer surfacer
7. • Allow to dry and apply guide coat
8. • Final sand with 500 grit by hand or DA w/interface pad
9. • Scuff wash
10. • Wash with soap and water
11. • Mask if needed
12. • Wipe with wax and grease remover

13. • Tack with tack cloth
14. • Spray with primer sealer
15. • Spray base
16. • Spray clear

Additional Resources

I have many additional resources that will be included at the end of this book. However, I do not want to include them under each module. As an instructor, I am aware that too much is not always a good thing. Information overload may leave you feeling behind, confused, and/or burned-out. Therefore, concentrate on the information and resources in each chapter. Once you have completed the book, you can explore the additional resources. Again, don't stress about getting through all of the additional resources all at once. Remember simplicity...keep it simple.

Module 11 Safety Quiz

Once you have completed the module content, take the module 11 quiz below. Please note that you must score 75% or higher to receive a certificate. This is a short quiz with only 10 questions. There is not a time limit set on this quiz so take your time. Find the correct answer if you do not know for sure. **The objective of this quiz is to help** you learn the information if you do not know the answer, not guessing. Good luck!

Additional Resources
You Will Need To Access This From The E-Book Format or the Members Website To Access The Links.

Module 1-Safety
1.   •EPA-Official EPA Website
2.   •Auto Body OSHA
3.   •3M™ 40 CFR Part 63 – Subpart 6H Training - 3M Course
4.   •July-August 1999, "Using A Fire Extinguisher"Official EPA Website - PDF
5.   •May-June 1995, "Welding-A Workplace Health Hazard" - PDF
6.   •National Fire Protection Association
7.   •National Institute for Occupational Safety and Health (NIOSH)
8.   •September-October 1996, Protecting Yourself From lsocyanates -Official EPA Website - PDF
9.   •May-June 1988, Paint Shop Hazards - PDF

Module 2-History
1.   •Collision Repair Overview - Sterlings PDF
2.   •Automobile History

Module 3-Metal Straightening - Steel
1.   •Express Damage Repair - 3M Course

2.   •<u>Large Damage Body Repair</u> - 3M Course
3.   •<u>Small Damage Body Repair</u> - 3M Course
4.   •<u>Stationary Auto Glass Removal &</u>
       <u>Installation</u> - 3M Course
5.   •<u>Corrosion and Coatings</u> - 3M Course
6.   •<u>I-Car Steel Repair</u> - PDF
7.   •<u>November 27, 2006</u>, "Exterior Panel
       Straightening-Part Two"
8.   •<u>November 15, 2006</u>, "Exterior Panel
       Straightening-Part One"
9.   •<u>January-February 1989</u>, "U.S. Car Makers-
       Guidelines For Use Of Heat" PDF
10.   •<u>July-August 1988</u>, "The Role Of Zinc In
       Corrosion Protection" PDF
11.   •<u>October 22, 2007</u>, "Steel Identification Using
       Hardness Testing"
12.   •<u>ST01A Stress-Relieving Heat Limitations</u>
       <u>(230.3 Kb)</u> PDF
13.   •<u>ST01S Stress-Relieving Heat Limitations</u>
       <u>(217.1 Kb)</u> PDF
14.   •<u>ST11 Structural Straightening (325.4 Kb)</u>
       PDF
15.   •<u>ST21A Metal Repair (324.0 Kb)</u> PDF
16.   •<u>ST21S Metal Repair (364.9 Kb)</u> PDF

Module 4-Body Fillers
  1.   •<u>Fibre Glass-Evercoat Video</u>

2. •ST31 Body Fillers (258.1 Kb) PDF
3. •July-August 1998, "Premium Body Fillers" PDF
4. •May-June 1997, "Dustless Sanding Systems" PDF
5. •November-December 1988, "New Body Fillers & What They Can Do For You" PDF
6. •July 19, 2004, "Repairing Hail Damage"

Module 5-Welding

1. •May-June 1998, "Heat Control When MIG Welding" PDF
2. •March-April 1995, "Temperature Indicators" PDF
3. •September-October 1990, "Welding Coated Steel" PDF
4. •July-August 1996, "Weld-Through Primers" PDF
5. •I-Car MIG Plug Welding - Steel PDF
6. •I-Car MIG Plud Welding - Aluminum PDF
7. •MIG Brazing facts about non-fusion
8. •Student Demonstration - Plug Weld
9. •September-October 1990, "Welding Coated Steel" PDF
10. •March-April 1990, "Cautions For Electronic Work" PDF
11. •November 22, 2004, "Open Butt Joint Welds"

Module 6-Plastic Repair

1. •Americas Plastics Council
2. •Saturn Plastic Repair Information
3. •SMC Repairs for the GM 200 Series Van
4. •PR01 Plastic Repair, Welding (358.1 Kb) PDF
5. •PR11 Plastic Repair, Adhesive (356.2 Kb) PDF
6. •November-December 1999, "Solving Plastic Adhesion Problems" PDF
7. •July-August 2000, "Repairing SMC Cargo Boxes" PDF
8. •March-April 1994, "How To Repair TPO" PDF
9. •July-August 1991, "Repairing Textured Plastic Surfaces" PDF
10. •November-December 1990, "Repairability And The New GM Saturn" PDF
11. •September-October 1990, "Q & A On SMC" PDF
12. •May-June 1990, "Repairing RRIM (Reinforced Reaction Injection Molding)" PDF
13. •November-December 1989, "Plastics In The Auto Market On The Increase" PDF
14. •November-December 1989, "SMC Repair Materials" PDF

15.   •September-October 1988, "Use Of Plastics On The Rise" PDF

Module 7-Preparation

1.   •Prime and Paint After Part is Sandblasted
2.   •Blend Panel Sanding - 3M Course
3.   •Dry Primer Sanding - 3M Course
4.   •Masking Best Practices - 3M Course
5.   •February 07, 2005, "Safe Use Of Ultraviolet-Cured Primer-Surfacers"
6.   •July 29, 2002, "Clarifying Sandpaper Grading"
7.   •December 02, 2002, "Repairing Spray-On Bed Liners"
8.   •February 04, 2002, "Roll-On Primer Surfacer"
9.   •September-October 1988, "Use Of Plastics On The Rise" PDF
10. •May-June 1993, Tinted Primers And Sealers PDF
11. •Car Masking PDF
12. •May-June 1997, Dustless Sanding Systems PDF
13. •May-June 1988, Self-Etching Primer Update PDF

Module 8 - Spray Guns

•   IWATA

- SATA
- DeVILBISS

Module 9 - Sealers, Paints, and Clears

1. • Three Stage Paint Guide
2. • RF01P Surface Preparation (393.7 Kb) PDF

3. • RF01S Surface Preparation (393.5 Kb) PDF
4. • RF11 Masking (200.1 Kb) PDF
5. • RF21 Finish Removal (262.6 Kb) PDF
6. • RF41 Finish Application (326.1 Kb) PDF
7. • RF81 Finish Defects (487.4 Kb) PDF
8. • July 02, 2008, "Vehicle refinishing, finding new ways to shine: part one"
9. • July 21, 2008, "Vehicle refinishing, finding new ways to shine: part two"
10. • August 18, 2003, "Overlooked Items That May Lead to a Color Match Problem"
11. • April 28, 2008, "Custom Painting – Beyond Traditional Finishes"
12. • October 21, 2002, "Clearcoat Blending Considerations"

Module 10 - Detailing

1. • Buffing and Removing Small Scratches

2. • <u>Meguiars How-To Videos</u>
3. • <u>Paint Finish Spot Panel</u>
4. • <u>Paint Finish Full Panel</u>
5. • <u>Vehicle Clean Up - Detailing</u>
6. • <u>Scotchgard™ Chemicals Application</u>
7. • <u>Headlight Lens Restoration</u> - 3M Course

Module 11 - Paint Defects

• <u>PPG PAINT DEFECTS</u>
• <u>Paint Defects</u> PDF

Bolt-on Panels

A Quick Overview

Vehicles are attached with various methods. We've briefly discussed weld-on panels, but there are also adhesives, clips, rivets, blots, and screws. In this lesson we're going to discuss panels that are attached with clips, rivets, nuts, bolts and screws.

Designs have changed quite a lot over the years. Older model cars required extensive adjusting skills to properly align the bolt-on panels. This was a good and bad thing. The good thing about is that there were enough adjustments to make body lines and gaps match up. However, too many adjustments could also become frustrating at the same time. Modern day cars have fewer adjustments. This is because unibody cars allow less tolerance. In other words, the structure must be properly aligned for the sheet metal to align. If you did not properly align the structure when pulling, it will show up after sheet metal is put on. So hiding bad frame work by aligning the sheet metal is not an option with unibody cars.

With that said, you are still going to have to align sheet metal and there are some rules to follow that will help you make the proper adjustments.

R&R - R&I
Bolt on panels are going to fall under two categories. The first is removing and replace (R&R). This is when parts will be removed and replaced with new or used parts. The other category it remove and install (R&I).

This is when you remove a part and install the same part back onto the vehicle. This is required when you may have to remove parts to access the damaged parts.

Trick for R&I

Many times when you are removing and installing the same part, it will have a paint mark or stains where the bolts were located. This makes it simple to place the bolts back to the same place that they were at before the part was removed. You can also use a grease pencil to mark the attachment points, which will give you a reference when re-installing the parts. This can same time and will only require minimum adjustment, if any, when installing parts. However, you will not have this advantage when replace with new parts. This may require additional aligning.

What do I align to?

This is something that you need to determine before starting the aligning process. If you are only changing one part; it's a simple process. However if you are replacing an entire side of a car, it can become more challenging. The sequence that you align your sheet metal must follow this order. Always start with what will not adjust. For example, let's remove all of the sheet metal from a car and re-install and align it. First you want to start with the door. If it is a four door, start with the rear door. This is because you must align it to the quarter panel and the rocker panel. Once the rear door is aligned to the quarter and rocker panel, you can now move to the front door and align it to the rear door and rocker panel. Then the fenders and hood. When aligning sheet metal that latch, such as doors, hoods, and deck lids, you also need to remove the latches or strikers. You want the part to align without latching. It is a common mistake to allow the latch or striker do the final adjusting, for example, moving the panel up, down, to the left or right making the alignment. We want the door to properly align without the help of the latch or striker. Then we can install and adjust the striker or latch to fit the door.

Now that we know this, we have the rear door aligned to the quarter and rocker, as they are stationary. Next, we adjusted the front door to the rear door and rocker panel. Next we can move to the front end. Install the fender, but only snug the bolts hand tight. This will allow you to do some fine adjustments. Now go ahead and align the back of the fender to the front of the door and snug them down. Care must be taken that you gap has enough clearance to clear the fender so paint will not be chipped off when opening the door. Once you have the rear of the fender aligned to the door, we can install the hood panel. Remember, we have not tightened up the front of the fender yet, so we can still make adjustments. But before aligning the fender to hood, you must align the hood to the cowl panel. The center the hood should properly align with the hood latch when installed. Now that the hood is installed, you can now align the front of the fender to the hood and tighten everything down. The bumpers or bumper covers and other front end pieces, such as lights, grills, etc, can be installed.

It is important that you follow this sequence. If not, you may find that the rear door will not properly align to the quarter panel....and you are not going to be able to make any adjustments to the quarter.

Gaps

Gaps are a give-away to people that something is wrong. Even the untrained eye can see uneven body gaps. Therefore, a great deal of time should be taken to assure the gaps are the same. There are gap measurement tools that will give you the exact measurement that a gap should be. However, paint sticks have helped me align many panels. The paint stick can be placed between the panels while the panel is tightened down. Depending on the gap, I have also used two paint stick placed on one another to help me create a wider gap.

Protect Edges

One thing that you will need to be extremely careful with is the panel edges. For example, if you bump the edge of a panel to the adjacent panel causing a scratch, you may have to repaint the part. This is especially true with fresh paint. One way to help eliminate this is to apply one or two layers of masking tape to the edge to protect the edges from being scratched or damaged.

Pre-Alignment

It is also important to test fit your panels before the final installation. The last thing that you want is to paint a fender and scratch it putting it one. By pre-fitting it, you can make the needed adjustments and tweak the fender if needed. This way, the fender will be a perfect fit when installed.

Making It Fit

It would be great if panels always fit perfect, but that is not a reality. This is especially true when working with aftermarket sheet metal. During the test-fit you may have to make minor adjustments to make the part fit properly. This may include slight shaping, twisting or whatever it takes to make it fit. This is why it's important to make your test fit and adjustments before painting the panel. This will prevent the headache of trying to make last minute tweaks, while trying not to damage the panel.

Paint the Panel on the Car

Some shops may prefer to paint the panel on the car. If this is the case, you can edge the panel, and then install it before painting. Once on the vehicle, the panel can be prepped and ready for paint. Depending on the repair shop or circumstances may determine if you paint the part on or off of the vehicle.

Painting Parts off Vehicle

The advantages of painting part off of the vehicles are: edge inside and paint outside of part at the same time, everything is stripped, moldings, trim, bolts, etc. This will result in a cleaner paint job. The obvious disadvantage is the extra care that must be taken when installing the part, as it has fresh paint. Many shops that concerned about lean or cycle times may use this system.

Painting Parts Installed

The advantages of painting parts on the car is that you will not chance damaging the fresh paint during installation. The disadvantages are having two separate spraying operations to get the part painted. For example, you will need to mix paint, spray paint, and clean the gun two times. Once during edging and once when painting the outside of the part.

Both methods will achieve a professional repair. It will just depend on procedures that that shop that you work at has set in place.

Shims

When panels had more adjustments, we used to used shims to help us align panels. This is a slotted piece of metal that could be place between the parts. For example, if the rear of the front fender is sitting low, you could place a shim between the fender and car body, which would set the fender higher. However, I do not see shims as much as I used to, but they can be a life saver if used sparingly.

The Dollar Trick

One way I was taught how to test door fits at the first dealership that I worked at was how to use a dollar to determine if a door closes properly. This is done by placing a dollar bill between the seals between the door and body, then pulling it out. If it pulls out too easy, then the door is too loose and adjustments must be made. If you were unable to pull the dollar out, then the door was too tight and adjusts must be made. The correct fit was when the dollar pulled out with a little force. The dollar techniques can be performed all the way around door checking fit.

Think It Through

The trick to aligning panels is to take your time and think about what adjustments that you have on each panel. Think about what all that certain adjustment will affect. For example, if move the lower door hinge on the body side forward towards the front of the car, you are going to tighten the gap between the door and fender, but also widen the gap between the front door and rear door, This will also lower the rear of the door, which may result in an height misalignment. Just think it through and try it. Panel alignment takes practice. It's going to take hands-on training to get the hang of it.

Clips

This is the one thing that aggravates me. I do not know why there cannot be some type of standardized clip variation, like there is with bolts and nuts. No, clips are complicated. There is always a new clip out there that you have to determine how to remove without breaking it, which is impossible sometimes. Once the clip is broke, you must order the clip if you do not stock them. I think it would be impossible to have every clip needed in inventory. However, more clips are being used on cars, so I should stop complaining and deal with it.

When removing clips, examine them first to determine how they are removed. If you just start yanking and pulling, you may damage the clips and the parts that you are removing. There are special clip tools that will help you remove clips without damaging them.

Bag It

This is a tip that will save you time and money in the end. Always bag your hardware. I have a funny story about this. I convinced the students working on a long project to bag everything. This was a car that was heavily damaged, and many different students worked on the car throughout the school year. Towards the end of school, we finally had the car repaired and ready to put back together. The students did a great job of bagging all of the hardware, but I realized that the bags were not labeled. We had a container full of bags, but this did not do us much good when we tried to determine what went where. Therefore, always label the bags too. For example, on one bag write right front fender. Then put all of the hardware to the right front fender into the bag. Have a separate bag for each part that you remove.

A Picture Is Worth A Thousand Words

I recommend to always do this, but if it is a quick job 1 or two days and you're the only one working on the car, you're probably going to remember where everything goes. However, if it is a long project or especially restoration jobs, this will help you considerably. Another thing that you may consider when taking parts off is to take a digital photo of the parts and use them as a reference when reassembling.

Store

Do not store parts in the car. This can create additional dirt and stains that will require cleaning at another time. Screws and parts on the floor board and/or seat may result in the hardware getting kicked or knocked out during the repair process. Some shops really frown on this and it a good habit to avoid. Therefore, store parts and hardware in designated containers. The best method is to use a rolling rack that can be moved with the car. That way, all parts and hardware will be in one place and you will know exactly where to get the parts when you are ready for them. For hardware, use a container and place the container on the cart.

Don't Throw Them Away Too Fast

Always keep the damaged parts until the job is completed. If you throw the parts away to soon, you may find that you forgot to remove a clip or molding off of the old part. You can also use the damaged parts as a reference if needed. Once the job is out the door, you can do whatever you want with the damaged parts.

New Parts

When your new parts come in be sure to inspect them for damage and make sure that it's the correct part. If the part is damaged, you may need to call the parts business that you ordered the part from and discuss it with them. I have had the business pick the damaged part up and brink another one, but they have also paid repair time as well. This will depend on your relationship the policies that the parts business has in place. If you are not familiar with the parts company or have never done business with them before, it would be a good idea to inspect the part while the delivery driver is still there. This will allow you to refuse the part on the spot and request a new one be sent.

Front Clip

Some cars and pick-ups (body over frame) allow you to replace the entire front end clip. When I used to purchase front clips, they would send me the bumper, header panel, (if it had one) grill, radiator, ac condenser, front fenders, and the hood. This worked great as you could take the front clip off as an assembly, not many bolts and remove the entire front assembly. Then you could make any necessary repairs and take the used clip that was purchased at a salvage yard and install the entire clip as assembly. This saves a lot of time when doing it this way. Make the adjustments that you need to align the fenders to the doors and tighten the bolts in the rear of the fenders. Now, with the radiator bolts still lose, you can shift the front end to the right or left to align the front end of the vehicle. That's it! It's a simple process. This is an option when there was a front end wreck damaging the grill, hood, and fenders.

That is a quick overview. The only other advice that I have concerning blot on parts is to do it. Like anything else, it going to take practice.

Industry Resources
You Will Need To Access This From The E-Book Format or the Members Website To Access The Links.

Airbag
1. •I-Car Airbag Information
2. •Changes in Head Restraint Requirements - PDF
3. •www.airbagsolutions.com

Auto Manufactures
• www.hondacars.com
• www.chrysler.com
• www.ford.com
• www.gm.com
• www.nissanusa.com
• www.toyota.com

Door Skins
1. •I-Car - Steel - PDF
2. •I-Car - Aluminum - PDF
3. •I-Car Plastic - PDF
4. •Evercoat Adhesive Video

5. •Outer Door Panel Bond Separation

Estimating

www.autodatalabels.com - Resource to purchase information labels

www.degweb.org - Website to submit estimating guide errors or concerns

www.safekids.com

P-Pages - PDF of the Mitchell P-Pages

3-Stage Paint: A Guide to Manufacturer's 3-Stage Colors

Best Practices - PDF

Full Frame

1.   • Full Frame: On the rack again

2.   •Frame Replacement on 1997-2001 Ford F-150 and F-250 Truck Models

3.   •1992-1995 Ford Econoline Front Horn Replacement

4.   •Full Frame Repair Recommendations - Good Training Resource

5.   •Dodge Ram 1500 4x4 Front Frame Horn Replacement

6. •1997-99 Ford 4x4 Truck Frame Horn Replacement

Learning, Articles, Tips, Resources

ALLDATA CollisionConnect

Auto Body SEO CONSULTANT - Chris Sheehy

Elite The Name You Can Trust For Automotive Professionals - Bob Cooper

OEM One Stop TechInfo Site

Tech-Cor

The National Automotive Service Task Force (NASTF)

www.vehicleinfo.com/articles.php
Uniform Repair Procedures For Collision Repair

Insurance Information/Customers' Rights

www.stopsteering.com

www.insurancegripe.com

www.autoclaimshelp.net

OEM Service Information

Free and Some Paid Resources

- www.serviceexpress.honda.com

- erwin.audiusa.com

- www.bmwtechinfo.com

- www.techauthority.com

- www.installers-mopar.com

- www.motorcraft.com

- www.motorcraftservice.com

- www.goodwrench.com/ServiceCenters/index.jsp

- www.gmtechinfo.com

- www.hyundaitechinfo.com

- www.infiniti-techinfo.com

- www.isuzusource.com

- www.jaguartechinfo.com

- www.kiatechinfo.com

- www.landrovertechinfo.com

- techinfo.lexus.com

- www.mazdaserviceinfo.com

- www.startekinfo.com

- www.minitechinfo.com

- www.mitsubishitechinfo.com

- www.nissan-techinfo.com

- techinfo2.porsche.com

- www.saabtechinfo.com
- www.gmtechinfo.com
- techinfo.subaru.com
- www.suzukitechinfo.com
- techinfo.toyota.com
- www.toyotapartsandservice.com
- erwin.vw.com
- www.volvotechinfo.com

Paint Refinish

1. •PPG Blending
2. •PPG OnlineTraining - Must be in their system
3. •Painting Plastics
4. •Effects of Acid Rain
5. •3-Stage Paint: A Guide to Manufacturer's 3-Stage Colors
6. •DuPont Procedures: A Guide to Manufacturer's Technical Information
7. •July 02, 2008, "Vehicle refinishing, finding new ways to shine: part one"
8. •August 18, 2003, "Overlooked Items That May Lead to a Color Match Problem"

9. •December 02, 2002, "Repairing Spray-On Bed Liners"

10. •November-December 1996, Shifting Colors - PDF

11. •April 22, 2002, "Waterborne Basecoats"

12. •November-December 2000, Spray Gun Control - PDF

13. •September-October 1997, Repair Those Door Chips - PDF

14. •January-February 2001, Spray Gun Fluid Tip, Needle, And Air Cap - PDF

15. •May-June 2000, Finishes And Refinishes In the 21st Century - PDF

16. •November-December 1992, Matching Three-Stage Finishes– Repair Procedures That Make The Job Easier - PDF

Paintless Dent Repair

1. •April 16, 2007, "Toyota lists Paintless Dent Repair (PDR) considerations"

2. •September-October 1999, "Another Look At Paintless Dent Repair"

3. •November-December 1999, "Another Look At Paintless Dent Repair- Part 2"

4. •May-June 1996, "The Art Of Paintless Dent Removal

Paint Manufacture Information

1. •Akzo/Nobel Car Refinishes
2. •BASF / Glasurit Automotive Refinishes
3. •DuPont Automotive Finishes
4. •PPG Industries, Inc.
5. •Sherwin Williams Automotive Finishes, Corp.
6. •House Of Kolor
7. •Kustom Shop
8. •Valspar Refinish
9. •Martin Senour

Parts Information

•www.parts.com

Steel Identification and Repair Considerations

1. •January-February 1989, "U.S. Car Makers-Guidelines For Use Of Heat"
2. •October 22, 2007, "Steel Identification Using Hardness Testing"

3. •September 11, 2007, "Recommended General Motors Steel Reparability Matrix"

Quarter Panel Replacement

QT01A Quarter Panel (262.0 Kb) - Aluminum - PDF
QT01P Quarter Panel (264.1 Kb) - Plastic - PDF
QT01S Quarter Panel (494.9 Kb) - Steel - PDF
QT11A Outer Wheelhouse (228.7 Kb) - Aluminum - PDF
QT11S Outer Wheelhouse (375.8 Kb) - Steel - PDF

Sectioning

1. •Ford Taurus Front Unirail Sectioning

2. •Index of Published Sectioning Procedures

3. •Important Repair Concerns when Sectioning Structural Components

Side Impact Collision

Side Impact Collision

Training

1. • 3M Training Videos - Online Training

2. • Collision Blast - Collision Repair Training Resource

3. • I-CAR

4. • <u>NATEF Collision Repair School Search</u>

5. • <u>Toyota Prius Service Precautions</u>

Instructor Resources

You Will Need To Access This From The E-Book Format or the Members Website To Access The Links.

Collision Repair Curriculum
Collision Repair Curriculum Guideline
Click here to download the NATEF 2009 Collision Repair & Refinish Program Standards in pdf format.
Click here to download the NATEF 2009 Collision Repair & Refinish Task List in Excel format.
Click here to download the NATEF 2009 task lists with changes highlighted in Word format.
Click here to download the NATEF 2009 tools & equipment lists with changes highlighted in Word format.
Curriculum PowerPoint
Rubric - Generic Rubric that can be edited

Recruiting Ideas
Gearing Up For the Next Generation - This is a pdf file from I-CAR that discusses the collision repair career pathway. Great to hand out as a recruiting tool.
Snapshot Of The Collision Industry - This is a pdf file from I-CAR that shows the statistic of the collision repair industry. National salary, ages, etc.

Prop Ideas
Props for Collision Training - This is ideas of props that you can use for your teaching. Most of these can be purchased from I-CAR; however, there are directions of how to build them yourself too.

Learning Styles

Bloom's Taxonomy: Original and Revised - This explains the different levels of learning
VARK Learning Style Test - A guide to learning styles
Question That Promote Deeper Thinking
Top 8 - Reason to set goals
What Is Contextual Learning

Classroom Management

Addressing The Skills Gap Through Career and Technical Education in New York City High Schools

Getting Results - this website offers 6 FREE modules with streaming videos to help you get better results in your classroom.

Randy Pausch Last Lecture: Achieving Your Childhood Dreams - Video

Study Guides and Strategies - This website is full of helpful information for helping students study.
My First Teach: A Trainers Life Behind The Scenes- Do you remember your first day of class? This article may jog a few memories that you had.

CNN Student News
This website is student news that you can start your class with. A good warm up to get the day started.

How Not To Use A PowerPoint - This is funny video of how NOT to make a PowerPoint

UCLA Plagiarism Tutorial - Bruin Success with Less Stress   This tutorial was created for UCLA students, but the topics are of academic dishonesty, citing sources, plagiarism, and file sharing

Development

Best Websites For Educators - PDF

Tip of the Week

What is a podcast video? - How To Podcast

5 Core Propositions

What Teachers Need To Know

Preparing Lesson Plans and Objectives
How To Write Clear Objectives
Writing Performance Objectives

Virtual
Interactive Training Demo - Here is an excellent interactive website that can be use to demonstrate suspension, brakes, etc.

Virtual Collision/Paint Shop- This is a cool interactive virtual paint and body shop.

Other Teaching Resources
Discovery Education
Edutopias
Gen X and Gen neXt.
Preparing Students For A Global Economy

I-Stream

League

StarLink

Classroom 2.0 - Online Social Network For Teachers

ACTE :: Association for Career and Technical Education

Qwiki - **Short Video Tutorials**

TeacherTube.com

Skills and Competencies Needed In The Work Place

Success Training

Training for the student/instructor, or employee/employer. Creating top results at school and/or in the work place.

Try to limit yourself to one lesson per week and take time each week to apply the lesson to your life.

Lesson 1

Explore and Discover Your Hidden Talents - It All
Starts With You

*"Great things are accomplished by talented people who
believe they will accomplish them." ~Warren G. Bennis*

Do you remember one time in your life that
someone believed in you? Maybe no one else did,
including you, but someone did. This resulted in
you believing in yourself and going on to make the
achievements that you made in life. If you have
never had this experience, I challenge you to look
inside yourself to explore, discover, and unlock
what may be hidden within you. If you have had
this experience, I challenge you to be that person
for someone else. Zig Ziglar talks about good
finders. People that find the good in others. Zig
gave the analogy of gold mining. You have to go
through tons of mud to find a little gold. Therefore,
look through other peoples faults to find that little
bit of good and help strengthen that quality that
they have.

This is the bottom line. It all comes down to you. If
you did not have someone help you build
confidence in yourself, don't use that as a crutch in
life. You cannot go through life blaming failures on
him or her or what did not happen in your life. To
be successful in life you need to learn to make
things happen with or without the help and support
of someone else. Better yet, if you want to be a
good leader, you need to be that person that helps

find the good in others. That is what produces top performers and champions in the workplace.

Please watch lesson 1 videos below, before continuing.

POINTS IN LESSON 1:

There are many people that have went through life never discovering or claiming all of their talents in life. Perhaps they feel cheated in life because they did not get the support that other people got. Or maybe they go through life always looking for someone to blame for all of their faults and failures. Well, I hate to be the one to break it to you, but life is not always fair. You must deal with your situation and overcome any obstacles in your path. You are really the only person in control of your success. It all start with you.

1) As a student or employee it is important to overcome all of life's challenges. I encourage you to stop accepting meritocracy, stop blaming others, and start exploring, discovering and claiming everything life has to offer you.

2) As a manager or teacher it is important to help each employee or student discover their talents and abilities. Whether you know it or not, you are a huge influence in their life. They are looking up to you for direction and leadership. You can the help them achieve success, but you also have the ability to help feed their excuses of why they can't succeed. You can contribute to being a positive or negative influence in your employees or students

life. I encourage you to be a good finder. If you do this, could you imagine how successful your students may become? Or how successful your business would be? This is what will take your business to the next level.

Assignment:

As a student, manager, leader, entrepreneur, or employee; take some time this week to think about what abilities you may have. Has anyone ever complimented you? Have you ever noticed that you've done something well? What are you passionate about?

1) Once you've discovered an ability that you have, post the talent you have to the comment section of this blog or email it to me.

2) Think of one way that you can use and strengthen your talent this week.

3) Do you see a talent or ability that one of your students, employees, children or spouse have? Give them a pat on the back then support and encourage them.

4) Please post or email me your results from this lesson.

Lesson 2

Facing The Giants To UNLOCK Your Power

"Just remember, you can do anything you set your mind to, but it takes action, perseverance, and facing your fears."
~Gillian Anderson

This post ties to the last post about unlocking your hidden talents and skills. We are going to expand on this topic this week, then we will move on to other topics. We'll also discuss how you need to keep an open mind and be willing to consider new things, and the last thing will be about the times you must face your giants (challenges in life) before you can overcome them.

First, let's talk about helping others unlock their talents. You do not have to be trained, have a fancy degree, be rich, or anything else to inspire someone else. If you go through life looking for the opportunity to make a difference in someone's life, I guarantee you will get your chance. Please note in the video, there was nothing special with the guy at the gas station. He was an average person with no special training. However, he was able to connect with the kid and make a difference in his life.

Second, always be willing to learn from others. It's like going to the grocery store. You plan to buy something or you would not have driven there. So you don't want to come out empty handed. However, you certainly do not want to come out with everything in the store either. You walk through the store getting the things you need and leave the things you don't need on the shelf. Life is the same way. We need to listen and be open to all ideas and use what you need. If you don't need it, leave it on the shelf. If the kid would not have listened to the guy at the gas station, he may not have ever unlocked his hidden talents.

Lastly, sometimes you must face the giants in your life. The giants are obstacles in your way of getting where you want to go. It's kind of like the saying "fight fire with fire." If you keep running from your fears, your fears will control you for the rest of your life. However, like the kid in the video, once you face your giant, that obstacles just became a stepping stone and you go on to new and better things. Go out there and help someone today. The opportunities are all around you. Co-workers, students, children, spouse....we all can use some encouragement. Be Sure To Watch This Video

Please watch lesson 2 videos below, before continuing.

Points In This Lesson:
1) Everyone needs to be willing to learn or keep an open mind. If the boy would not have accepted the

guys advice, he may never faced the bully and overcame his fear.

2) Everyone will have many challenges to face. It is necessary to face your challenges to overcome them. I have a quote that I like to use which is, "Challenges Produce Champions." In the story in this lesson; this quote makes a lot of sense as Carols did become a world champion. You must face and overcome your challenges as well if you want to become a champion in the workplace.

3.   3)If you are a business owner, manager, or teacher, this lesson has another point to consider. You don't have to be trained, have a fancy degree, or have a lot money to make a big impact in someone's life. If a gas attendant can make that big of a difference in a little boy's life, how big of an impact can you have with your employees or students? If you reach out and help someone become a top performer; this will benefit your company or team as well. Who would not want top performers on their team or company?

Assignment:
If you still have challenges that you need to overcome, I challenge you to face them and determine how you can overcome them. Take some time this week to reflect on your life to think of something that may be holding you back from being the person you really want to be. Once you identified the challenge, determine why you are afraid to face this challenge. Many times you will realize the reasons for fear are not really that

significant. For example, you may be afraid of what people will think. First of all, who are these people. If they are your family or employees, they should support you. If they are not family, friends, or employees, who cares what they think in the first place. Many times we may not really even be able to identify who those people are. Therefore, overcoming your fear becomes quite easy as you realize that all of your fears were false. If you still have a fear, determine if overcoming the challenge will make you more successful in the end.

1) Think of a challenge in your life and think of a way to overcome it. Please post your challenge in the comments section or email it to me.

As a manager, teacher, or leader look for opportunities to help others. Look for talents and abilities in others and reach out to help them discover and strengthen the talents. The more people you help the more successful your company or team will become.

2) I'm sure that you have already made a difference in someone's life before. Reflect on how that made you feel and leave us a comment or email me. Continue to look for opportunities to help people succeed. Because when they succeed so will you.

Lesson 3

A Business Lesson From Baseball

We've spent a lot of time at the baseball park this year. Our twin boys play, luckily they're on the same team, about twice a week. They are doing good this year. I believe that they have won 7 and lost 2.

One of the problems many of the kids have is striking out. However, not because they are swinging, but because they don't swing; they watch the ball go right by them. I hear the coaches encourage them to swing. If you make a strike by swinging, it will be all right. However, if you don't swing, then it is certain that you will not hit the ball and have a chance of hitting a home run.

One of the best known players of all times is Babe Ruth. He is known for his extremely high record of hitting home runs. However, you may not know that he struck out more than most players as well. He realized that if he plans to hit a home run, then he must swing the bat and give it his all.

The lesson in baseball is to take the risk or chance and swing the bat. You may strike out, but you may make a home run too.

Fun Fact: Babe Ruth struck out 1,330 times and hit 714 Home runs in his career in 8,399 at bats.

The same lesson can apply to business success. I think as a kid, we become scared to take risks. (if I swing I may strikeout!) It's safer to not take chances and we grow up afraid to take risks. It is easier to stay in our comfort zones and "walk" or coast through life. However, the risk takers, shakers, movers, and people that can think outside of the box, are the people that can achieve the greatest (home run) success.

The lesson in baseball and business is this:

Make Wise Choices

• Baseball - Don't swing at everything. A good ball player knows when to swing and when the pitch is not worth swinging at.
• Business - Don't jump at every opportunity or deal - Make sure the opportunity or business deal is a good investment, a good decision and worth your time and effort. There are a lot of bad pitches and bad business deals or scams out there--be careful.

Keep your eyes on the ball
• Baseball - You must keep your eye on the ball if you plan to hit it. By taking your eyes of the ball, your chances of hitting the ball are slim.
• Business - Stay focused on your goals, purpose and the mission of your business. Focusing on too many things or things that will not benefit your business will limit your success. Determine what is

important and don't allow yourself to focus on anything else.

Swing
• Baseball - When the pitch is a good one, SWING! If you don't swing, then it's certain that you will not hit the ball or make a home run. Don't worry if you swing and miss. If it is a good pitch, then it will be a strike anyway. Go out swinging!
• Business - When you determine that there is a good business deal go for it. Timing is important to being successful. Hesitation or procrastination will lead to many missed opportunities. There are no guarantees in life, but you will never be successful if you don't try.

In baseball and in life, I think the key point is to do you absolute best. Do your best at all you do. Whether at work, baseball, homework, or whatever; do your absolute best. Just like Bake Ruth, he gave it is all.

Here is a mentor of mine, Chip Foose, that is giving his advice to students at a college career day. I believe is some the best advice you will ever hear so be sure to watch this video.

Please watch lesson 3 videos below, before continuing.

ASSIGNMENT
1) Reflect on a time that you saw an opportunity and pursued it. You may have succeeded or you

may have failed, but leave us a comment or email me your results.

2) Think of a time that an opportunity presented itself to you and you reclined to pursue it. Was it a wise choice now that you look back at the opportunity? Share with us.

I know fear is an obstacle for some people, but it is an illusion to me. Failure always made me try harder next time. ~Michael Jordan

Lesson 4

Are You A Good Manager Or A Good Leader?

"Outstanding leaders go out of the way to boost the self-esteem of their personnel. If people believe in themselves, it's amazing what they can accomplish." ~Sam Walton

A study at Cornell University's Johnson Graduate School of Management found that compassion and building teamwork will be two of the most important characteristics business leaders will need for success a decade from now.

Managers and leaders are very similar in many ways, but they have different ways of accomplishing the same goal. Some managers are also excellent leaders, but there are some outstanding managers that do not possess the leadership skills. Let's take a minute to differentiate the two. Both leaders and managers have followers, but the leaders followers, follow by choice while the managers followers, follow because they must obey the manager. Managers do things right by following the book, while leaders do the right thing by their own intuition. Managers are more likely to work their way up the corporate ladder with experience and hard work. Leaders may shoot to the top with their enthusiasm, direction and vision they have for the company. We need a mixture of leaders, managers and followers to be successful. Leaders give direction, managers execute, and followers do. Therefore, the ability to be able to utilize each skill when needed is the key.

An example of a good leader is Martin Luther King. He had many followers that believed in him and his endeavors. I'm sure all of us have watched one of those cop movies where the cop goes outside their boundaries, uses "outside the box thinking," and may even get suspended for doing the right thing. They always get rewarded and become the leader and hero of the movie. You may be asking yourself, who are the followers? Well, everyone watching the movie is counting on the cop to do the right thing. In reality, we may not always come out the winner being a good leader. The movie Freedom Writers is a true story about a teacher that uses her leadership skills to earn the trust of her students; however she was not very well liked by her co-workers and was constantly challenged by her endeavors. However, she reached her goal of connecting with the students. She knew what her goal was and had to stay focused to achieve it.

A good example of a good manager is Donald Trump. I don't know his bio, but according to personality on "The Apprentice" he is a good manager. His followers follow him because he is "Donald Trump." If they don't follow him; "You're Fired." I am sure he has some leadership skills to get to where he is, but I think management is his stronger side in my opinion. It's easy to see with all his possessions that he does things right in the business world.

Two names pop into my head when I think of someone that possesses both leadership and management skills. They are Bill Gates and Sam Walton. These are two corporate giants who must have good management skills to get where they got and was/is liked and respected by many people.

I think we all can portray some of both qualities. However, we are probably naturally stronger or better in one area than the other. For example, you may be a good leader, but have issues executing the task at hand. Therefore, more attention to your management skills may be needed. I think it is important to discover our natural abilities and improve our lesser abilities to become great managers, leaders, teachers, or parents.

Please watch lesson 4 videos below, before continuing.

Lesson:
Everyone can become a great manager and leader. However, you are naturally stronger on one of the two styles. The key is to identify your natural abilities and develop you lesser abilities.

Assignment:
Determine if you are a stronger manager or leader. Do you do things right or do the right thing? Do people follow your lead because they have to or because they want to? Are you better at giving direction to a project or executing the task at hand?

1) Once you have determined your stronger ability, please leave a comment in the comment section of this blog or email me which one it is.

2) Then list one step you are going to take to improve your lesser ability. Please share your results so we can all learn from each other.

3) Think of all the presidents that we've had on history. Which one was the best leader? Which one was the best manager?

Here is a link to a test that will help you determine your qualities.

"The key to successful leadership today is influence, not authority." ~Ken Blanchard

Lesson 5

Focusing On Others To Achieve Success

"A leader is best when people barely know he exists, when his work is done, his aim fulfilled, they will say: we did it ourselves." ~Lao Tzu

I recently started reading a book titled "Co-Active Coaching." This book was written to help coach people towards success in work and in life. I've already read a few parts that I would like to share with you and expand on. I believe that some of the methods mentioned in this book can be used for coaching, teaching, and even building your business. The first thing that caught my attention was this**, "The coach does not deliver the answer; the coach asks questions and invites discovery."** This method of coaching allows the agenda to come from the employee or student, not the coach. The coach helps the employee or student to reach their goals by helping them discover and achieve their own goals, not the goals of the coach. This allows each coaching session to be tailored to the each employee or student's needs.

In education, we may say it like this**, *From the sage on the stage to the guide on the side.*** In other words, turning your learning environment

251

from a teacher led to a student led environment. The teacher led method has been used for many years, which is the teacher giving all of the lectures and the students listening and memorizing the material. However, many times the students learn the lesson long enough to ace a test, but forget the material shortly after. The student led model allows the instructor to force the students to lead, which requires the students to engage in the lesson and search and discover how to learn the material them self. The teacher is now more of a facilitator, which helps guide the students in the right direction. This allows more room for interactive and discovery discussions in the classroom.

Building Your Business When building a business you can use this method to build your team. You may want to build your business a certain way, but that does not mean everyone will want to do it exactly the same way you do. Just because I like to blog, does not mean that everyone will want to blog to market their business. Therefore, spending hours teaching them to blog is useless. They may want to use twitter to market their business. Therefore, time would be much more effective helping them with twitter. If you're a business owner, have an open mind. If the employee is achieving the desired end result, let them do it their way. Remember, there is always more than one way to get from A to B. I would never want to jeopardize quality, but if the end result is to your satisfaction, give them a little slack. You may be surprised of how productive your employees may become if they feel that they use their talents and abilities to contribute to the success of the company.

I recently started reading a book titled "Co-Active Coaching." This book was written to help coach people towards success in work and in life. I've already read a few parts that I would like to share with you and expand on. I believe that some of the methods mentioned in this book can be used for coaching, teaching, and even building your business. The first thing that caught my attention was this**, "The coach does not deliver the answer; the coach asks questions and invites discovery. "** This method of coaching allows the agenda to come from the employee or student, not the coach. The coach helps the employee or student to reach their goals by helping them discover and achieve their own goals, not the goals of the coach. This allows each coaching session to be tailored to the each employee or student's needs.

In education, we may say it like this*, From the sage on the stage to the guide on the side.* In other words, turning your learning environment from a teacher led to a student led environment. The teacher led method has been used for many years, which is the teacher giving all of the lectures and the students listening and memorizing the material. However, many times the students learn the lesson long enough to ace a test, but forget the material shortly after. The student led model allows the instructor to force the students to lead, which requires the students to engage in the lesson and search and discover how to learn the material them self. The teacher is now more of a facilitator, which helps guide the students in the right direction. This allows more room for interactive and discovery discussions in the classroom.

Building Your Business When building a business you can use this method to build your team. You may want to build your business a certain way, but that does not mean everyone will want to do it exactly the same way you do. Just because I like to blog, does not mean that everyone will want to blog to market their business. Therefore, spending hours teaching them to blog is useless. They may want to use twitter to market their business. Therefore, time would be much more effective helping them with twitter. If you're a business owner, have an open mind. If the employee is achieving the desired end result, let them do it their way. Remember, there is always more than one way to get from A to B. I would never want to jeopardize quality, but if the end result is to your satisfaction, give them a little slack. You may be surprised of how productive your employees may become if they feel that they use their talents and abilities to contribute to the success of the company.

Please watch lesson 5 videos below, before continuing.

LESSON
The main point of this lesson is to focus on the person you're helping and not your own concerns or agenda. This may not work in every instance,

but knowing when to lead and when to listen and direct or point someone in the right direction is the key to being a great coach, leader, manager, or teacher.

Learning involves levels. As you can see in the diagram, memorizing something long enough to do well on a test is just level one learning. At this level it is necessary that the manager or teacher give direction and tell them what needs to be done and how to do it. After repetition of doing the job or task the new employee will start to understand why they are doing it the way you instructed them. This stage still requires direction and supervision. Then they will move into the applying and analyzing stages. in These stages the employee is competent, but still require a little supervision. The evaluation stage is where they may make a mistake, but he or she will be competent enough to figure what went wrong. (learn from mistakes) The deepest or last level of learning is creating. This is when you need to step back and allow your employee to create their own style. (no one likes to be micro-managed) Always be available for questions and coach them, but try to allow them develop their own way of getting to the end result. So when the employer hires a new employee, there will be many hats the manager must wear to produce this type of results.

I guarantee you that effort and steps will pay you back in the end and allow the manger more time to do other productive tasks.

Assignment
1) It is very easy to dictate and voice your opinions. However, spend some time this week looking for the right opportunities to listen at a deeper level and help someone by guiding them. Think of questions that that will help point the person you helping in the right direction.
2) If you have a method that is working well let us know about it. Let's work together to produce the ideal employees.

Please leave us a comment or email me your results.

"You can have everything you want in life, if you help enough other people get what they want" ~Zig Ziglar

Lesson 6

Natural Born Leaders - Is There Any Hope For Me?

"Leaders are made, they are not born. They are made by hard effort, which is the price which all of us must pay to achieve any goal that is worthwhile." ~ **Vince Lombardi**

I'm sure you've heard that there are "natural born leaders." Does this mean that if you are not born with the traits (intelligence, self-confidence, determination, integrity, sociability; as described in the text "Leadership: Theories and Practices") that you cannot be a good leader.

It is true; some people are born with qualities which make it easy for them to be a leader. However, this statement is not an absolute. Some of the people that have the abilities to be a leader don't use their talents to do so. On the other hand I'm sure we have all witnessed a great leader that did not have any of the abilities mentioned above. What then makes leaders, leaders and followers, followers?

Even though some individuals are "natural born leaders" we can all learn to become leaders. While it comes natural for some people by their traits, looks, or personalities; others can learn the skills to become effective leaders as well. They just may

257

have to work harder to achieve the same results. For example, in school we see students that ace class without ever taking a book home and we see other students that ace classes struggling with late nights of homework. Same result, but different efforts to produce the same result.

With that said, we don't all have to be leaders. It takes a good mixture to make society productive. We need leaders to give the direction, managers to make sure it is done right, and followers to do it. If we were all leaders and agreed on the direction; there would be no results if there were no followers to do it. However, it may be necessary for us to change rolls according to our situations. For example, an employee may not enjoy being put on the spot, answering questions, or dealing with the public at work. They may simply like to show up to work, do their job, and go home. This employee would be considered a follower at work. However, when he arrives home he must become the leader to properly parent his or her children. So I think we must all strive to do our best in all areas of our lives in order to achieve our goals and dreams.

Here is an article over the **5 traits of a leader** that you may be interested to read.

Please watch lesson 4 videos below, before continuing.

Lesson: We can all be effective leaders, but we must all be good and good followers in life. The key is to know when to lead and when to follow. Just like teachers, there are time we must become we must become the student in order to learn and stay updated with the latest trends and techniques.

Assignment: Think of a time that required you to be a leader. What did you have to do to be an effective leader? What is one step that you can take to become a better leader this week? Please post comment or email me your results.

Lesson 7

Social Networking

Tell Your Story - The Key To Success

1.   •<u>The Link To Wall Drug Store</u>

Have you ever watched American Idol and noticed the Coke cups sitting on the counter? Coke pays a lot of money to have their cups sitting there, but don't you thing everyone already knows about Coke? Well, Coca-Cola knows how to brand a company and they understand the significance of keeping their product in front of their customers. Did you know that more people choose Pepsi in a blind taste test? However, when they can see the products more people pick Coke. This proves the power of branding.

With this said, I encourage you to consider getting your name or company out there in front of people more. It has never been easier or cheaper to do than now with social networking.

If you blog you may not to watch this next video. The video below shows you how to start our own blog absolutely free.

Please watch lesson 7 videos below, before continuing.

260

Your lesson this week is to add a comment on this blog with your new blog. Or if you already have a blog, please leave us a comment with a link to your blog.

Lesson 8

Time Management - Balancing Work and Life

Welcome to the Final Lesson of this 8-week course. I hope that you found some value from the eight lessons. If you will apply the eight different lessons to your life, business or classroom, I guarantee you that it will help you succeed in business and in life.

We covered lessons on self development, coaching, leadership, social media, and time management.

You will need to watch the video to complete lesson 8

Thanks Again For Completing The Business Success Training Course. Kudos To You My Friend. Now Go Put It All To Use.

Resources

Videos
- **Lesson 1 Videos**
- **Lesson 2 Videos**
- **Lesson 3 Videos**
- **Lesson 4 Videos**
- **Lesson 5 Videos**
- **Lesson 6 Videos**
- **Lesson 7 Videos**
- **Lesson 8 Videos**

Career Information

You Will Need To Access This From The E-Book Format or the Members Website To Access The Links.

Appraiser Information
ASA Code of Ethics
Bureau Department of Labor - Career Info
Collision Career Video
Collision Repair Passion Story
CareerOneStop
Finding Your Passion In Collision Repair
O*Net - Career Info.
SCRS Collision Repair Code Of Ethics
Work Options Videos
How To Become ASE Certified - An ASE Study Guide
PDF
NATEF Accredited Collision Repair Schools

Collision Repair Organizations
Automotive Service Association (ASA)
ASE Certification
I-CAR
Collision Repair Education Foundation
NATEF

A Career In Collision Repair

This course is to help you perform auto body and paint repair as a hobby, provide knowledge, refresh what you already know, etc. However, it is also designed to help those who are interested in pursuing a career in collision repair. I recommend that you take what you have learned in this course and apply it towards furthering your education in collision repair. I don't believe just reading a book or taking a course is enough training to enter the workforce as a profession as there is still a lot to learn. However, this training will give you the advantage and allow you to excel in a collision repair training program. I also recommend that you seek a part-time job in an auto body shop while attending college. I have noticed the students who work in the industry while attending college have a greater appreciation for the training and tend to outperform the students that do not work in the industry part time.

I am a collision repair instructor for a community college. If you live in the Wichita, Kansas area than I invite you to visit me about attending our collision repair program at Butler Community College. However, this course is designed to help you find a college that fits your needs, not a recruitment tool for one specific college. Therefore, I am going to discuss several types of schools and some of the differences between them. I am also going to give you a few recommendations of what to look for when considering a school to attend.

Private Schools

Private schools are not funded by state or federal. Therefore the full tuition is paid by the students, resulting in more cost to the students, rather than the government. Another disadvantage of attending a private school is that there credits do not transfer well with many other institutions if the student decides to further their education at a later time. The advantages of private schools is that they usually have specialty courses that further explore niches, such as custom fabrication and custom paint. Private schools appear to have more connection in the industry, as they are training students from many different demographical areas.

Community Colleges

Community colleges are funded by federal and state dollars. This results in less expense to the student. Some community colleges focus on smaller classroom sizes, which allows more one-on-one instructor/student time. One advantage, which can also be a disadvantage is that community colleges and adjust their curriculum to meet the needs of the community they serve. This provides top candidates for the community, but may be less effective in other demographical areas. Most community colleges that offer collision repair offer a certificate and an associate degree in collision repair. Credits are easier accepted by other institutions if you decide to further you education at a later time.

Technical Colleges

There are also technical colleges that focus on technical careers. I believe they are funded by the government. However, I am less familiar with this type of education. I attended WyoTech (private) and now teach at a community college. Therefore, I have not had much exposure to technical colleges. I am not going to give advantages and disadvantages on a technical college. However, this is an option for you to consider.

Public Schools

There are also some public schools that offer collision repair as a technical elective. The advantages of this are obvious. The only cost to the students are the required lab fees, tools and safety gear. This is by far the less expensive way to get started in this career pathway. Some public schools will even partner with colleges to provide the training. If you are interested in this career pathway, and your school offers this type of training, I highly encourage you to enroll. You must take the class seriously. You are receiving a free education that most other individuals are paying for.

To Find NATEF Accredited Collision Repair Programs In Your Area, Visit <u>NATEF</u> and click on Auto Body and Your State.

Tips When Considering A School To Attend

Why choose collision repair as a career pathway?

Hands-on: Why should your job be boring and dreadful? You can earn income doing the things you like to do. If you're someone that likes working with your hands, a high-tech environment and you enjoy being able to step back and see the results of your work; then collision repair may be a good fit for you.

High income potential: I-Car Education Foundation completed a survey, showing the average income that a collision repair technician earns. You may be surprised that the average income of $51,312 is higher than many other comparable trades. In fact, the top 10% earn $88,460. Although, just like with any career, you shouldn't expect this your first year on the job. These are the incomes you can expect to make with experience and commitment.

Job Security: As roads and highways become more populated with vehicles, the results are more auto accidents. Unfortunately, the automotive industry is not finding enough trained technicians to properly repair these modern day vehicles. This means job security for you.

Work will never be outsourced: Think about it! Could you imagine a damaged vehicle being loaded on a ship, taken overseas, repaired, and shipped back to the customer...it's not going to happen. We need trained collision and paint technicians right here in the United States, in every state and every city to repair our cars. As a technician, you will never have to worry about your job being outsourced.

What are some of the things to consider when choosing a school to attend?

NATEF certified: Make sure the school is a National Automotive Technician Education Foundation (NATEF) accredited. This gives you peace of mind knowing that the school has met the NATEF standards and is a quality school. NATEF is national recognized in the automotive industry and will give you a competitive edge, when you pursue a job. In order to be NATEF accredited, all instructors must be Automotive Service Excellence (ASE) certified to teach. This means that you will have competent instructors to ensure your success in the future.

I-Car affiliation: I am not claiming that a program must use I-CAR curriculum to be considered a top program, but it's an extra perk for you to consider. I-Car is an organization that helps the collision industry with on-going training. They provide training to technicians already on the job and they provide curriculum and support to colleges and technical schools to prepare students for the world-of-work. I-Car is known throughout the collision industry and will give your potential employer another perk to hire you by having obtained I-CAR points while in school.

Where do I find a school like this and how do I enroll?

1. Call the school to set up a time you can visit with them and ask to tour the collision repair program.
2. Is the collision program accredited? If so, who are they accredited through?
3. Are they affiliated with I-Car and what curriculum do they use?
4. Ask if one of the program instructors are available to speak with. You can ask them program specific questions. This will give you a better feel of the program and the instructors.
5. What is their student per instructor ratio? Are you more comfortable in large or small groups?
6. Find out what requirements, tools, tuition, and fees are required.
7. Have them explain the difference between a certificate and an associate's degree. (some technical schools and private schools may not offer associates degrees)
8. Does the college have any articulation agreements with any other schools, which allows the student to transfer into a four-year university?
9.   9.Once you feel you have made the correct decision, ask them to direct you to an advisor. The advisor will walk you through the steps to get you enrolled.

Here is my challenge to you when enrolling into a collision repair or any career.

The Challenge

The challenge is not just to enroll into the exciting collision repair technology programs, which offer a rewarding, lucrative and challenging career, but to enroll with the intentions of learning and applying what you learn to become a top performer in the automotive industry. I read a quote by Laurence J. Peter that makes a lot of sense to me. "Going to church doesn't make you a Christian any more than going to the garage makes you a car." The same stands true for education. Simply knowing how to do something is useless if you're not willing to use what you know to do it. Another example is like looking at a road map. You can look, read and study a map all day or even all year on how to travel from here to Texas. You may discover all the alternate routes you could travel, but unless you get into your car and drive there, you are still here in Kansas. Just knowing the information will not get you there, just like reading the Atkins Diet book will not make you lose weight. You must apply what you learn to reap the benefits.

The challenge is to enroll in a program, have an interest in collision repair technology, have good attendance, have a good attitude, be a team player, and be willing to learn and apply what you learn in order to become the champion of your trade. You may be saying "Yeah right!" Well, if that's your attitude that is what will always separate you from the doers, leaders and champions. The world is full of half doers and slackers. When they see a challenge they turn the other way and run. They show up to class just to receive the minimum grade to slide through or go to work just to receive a paycheck. However, top performers have a different mindset. They understand all the efforts they apply will reward them for the rest of their life. They are willing to stay focused on a goal until they have reached it. They fight hard for what they believe in, but pick their battles wisely. They see limitations and obstacles as challenges to overcome, not excuses to fail. They get back up when knocked down, instead of claiming that the challenge at hand can't be done. They base their future goals on what can be done, instead of focusing on their past failures. And they're always willing to help others up instead of laughing at them while they're down. These are the individuals who will be at the top of their careers, with the successful jobs, earning a lot of money, and having enough income to do all the things they desire.

According to I-Car the national average income for a collision technician earns over $51,000 and the top 10 % of technicians make over $88,000 a year. Many technicians even decide to start and operate their own successful business leaving the earning potential unlimited. Are you going to be successful or are you someone that will scrape by to make ends meet? The choice is yours. The things and values you consider success are up to you. Your teachers, parents, or friends can't make these choices for you. It's all up to you. If you're a slacker you can change. If you were not an honor student in school, you can improve and still become successful. If you have limitations you can overcome them. However, no one can help you if you are not willing to let them. If you're not willing to learn, to work hard, to complete assigned tasks, to help others, be present and on time, or to stay up with the fast paced changes and challenges of technology, than this industry is not a good fit for you. This program will be a waste of your time and a waste of our time. You may need to consider another career that does not require the physical application and challenges this industry requires. However, if you are willing to enroll in this career with the mindset of a champion, then we dare you to take the ultimate challenge that collision repair technology has to offer you.

~Donnie Smith
Dare to take the challenge!
"Challenges Produce Champions"

Auto Estimating

Part 1 - What Is An Estimate

Auto Repair Estimates are called different things including damage report, damage estimate, auto estimate, or several other names, but they are all basically the same thing. However, a damage estimate is more than just a sheet of paper listing the total cost of repair on it. An estimate is a <u>contract</u> or an agreement between two people. Just like with real estate, the owner and buyer must agree on a price and sign a contract of their agreement. A damage estimate is the same way in many ways, as there should be an agreement between the shop and customer and the customer should sign the agreement to authorize the shop to repair the vehicle. One thing that you need to explain to the customer, which is misunderstood many times, is that the total amount is just an estimate. Auto repair estimates do not guarantee the exact amount of the final invoice. There may be hidden damage or many other factors that may change before the car is completed. As an estimator, it's your job to have excellent communications with the customer. You need to let them know that an estimate is subject to hidden damage. You must also understand that the estimate or signed agreement is only good for items that are written on the estimate. If any additional work is needed, you will need to contact the customer and agree on the new amount. This is called a supplement, which may include additional parts or labor as needed.

Methods Used To Write Estimates

We used to write all auto repair estimates by hand using Mitchell Estimate Guides. This involved writing all of the damage on an estimate and looking in the estimating guide to get all of the parts prices and labor needed to estimate the job. Computer generated estimates have simplified and taken over the hand written estimates, but when learning how to estimate, I believe it to be crucial to learn all of the basics first, which requires estimating guides, a blank estimate, and a pen. Learning to hand write estimates is the foundation of becoming an effective estimator. Just like every house or building must have a strong foundation, an estimator must master the basics first.

The Sequence of an Estimate

Most estimating guides and computer systems are set up with the same sequence: starting with the front bumper cover and ending with the back bumper. This is important to know as you want to write the estimate in the same order to write a clean sheet. For example, if you are writing an estimate on a car that has damage in the front end, start with the front bumper and move towards the back of the car one part at a time. Bumper cover, front grill, right front fender, etc. Now when you use the guide it will be easy to follow along adding the prices and labor times.

Who Needs Estimators?

Every shop will need someone to write estimates for the customers. Some shops may have more than one estimator. Insurance needs the assistance of estimators as well. When you work for an insurance company writing auto repair estimates your title may be auto estimator or auto appraiser.

Part 2 - Adding Non-Included Operations To The Estimating Guide

Once we have all of the information needed from the vehicle we can take the estimate into the estimating office or area where we can complete and total the auto estimate. The estimating guide will provide a list of the parts with diagrams, the price of the parts, the flat rate labor to replace the parts (judgment time is not-included in the estimating guides; we'll discuss judgment time later) and the refinish flat rate to paint the parts if needed.

Parts and Abbreviations

It is very important to know the nomenclature of the parts and the abbreviations of the parts. You must also realize that parts may be called different things. A door outer repair panel may be how the guide describes what we know in body shop jargon, door skin. However, it is going to make it difficult to find the right parts if you do not have a clue what they are called. A couple of abbreviations that I am going to mention are R&I, which stands for remove and install. This is when you remove a part and put the same part back on. For example, there may not be any damage to a door, but it may have to be removed to gain access to the damaged area. Therefore, you will not have to remove the trim panel, glass, door handle, etc. This will be less flat rate than to replace the door. If you replace the door that is called R&R, which stands for remove and replace. Now you will have to transfer all of the hardware from the old door to the new door, which is going to take more time. Many times on front bumper covers and other assemblies they have an O/H, which stands for overhaul. This basically gives you time to take the assembly completely apart and to put it back together.

P-Pages
Look at your p-pages and learn all of the abbreviations. This is something that will help you. You don't just want to memorize what they stand for, but you want to understand what each abbreviation includes or does not include in the tasks.

Think About Wal-Mart When Writing Estimates
What is included and what is not included in each operation? This is something that you need to ask yourself every time you add a line to your estimate. This is where most mistakes are made when writing an estimate, which results in dollars lost for the shop. There are tons of non-included operations that go unclaimed on most estimates. Many times the estimator claims they do not put it on the estimate because the insurance company will not pay for it. There is some truth behind this story, but it is usually because they did not write it on the estimate correctly. You must itemize each procedure if you plan to get paid for it. It is like going to Wal-Mart. Have you ever gone to Wa-Mart and gathered a bunch of items in your cart, then went to check out; then they give you the

amount, which almost gives you a heart attack? Well, let's take this one step further; what if they gave you a receipt with just the total amount on it? You would probably claim that they made a mistake. However, when you get the itemized receipt, you look it over and realize all of the prices are correct. It just added up to more than you thought it would. I don't know if this has ever happened to you, but it happens to me all of the time. Insurance adjusters are the same way. If it is not crystal clear what you are charging for, they want to claim that it is not right and they do not want to pay that amount...I sure wish I could do that at the store! However, if you have every item listed separately and not bulged together, they can see that your charges are legitimate. So to determine what non-included operations you can add to your estimate, look in your p-pages. This will list everything that is included and everything that is not included. I recommend that you take some time and study the p-pages and know them by heart.

Part 3 - Getting Paid For The Non-Included Item

Get Paid For What You Do

If you write auto repair estimates for a body shop and you're not looking though all of your non-included items in your p-pages, you are leaving a lot of money unclaimed. These are operations that must be performed to complete the job. Therefore, the shop and the technician should get paid for it.

What Do Insurance and the IRS Have In Common?

Insurance companies are a lot like the IRS. There are many things that the insurance companies are willing to pay for just like the IRS has many tax saving benefits for businesses. However, if you don't ask for it, neither one of them will offer to give it to you. I am not saying that the insurance companies will pay you for everything you ask for, but it is certain you will not get paid for the operation if you don't ask for it. There may be as much non-included time on a part as the time given to R&R it. Let's take a look at an example.

The P-Pages

If you Google Motor Guide to Estimating, you will see the p-pages for CCC Pathways. There, you can see the included and not included items for each operation. If you look up a front fender you will see this listed:

Included Operations Include

1. •Align to vehicle
2. •Fillers (if mounted to fender)
3. •Cornering lamps (if mounted to fender)
4. •Fender liner
5. •Scoop
6. •Side marker
7. •Side repeater lamp

Non-Included Operations Include

1. •Antenna
2. •Bumper R&I
3. •Battery
4. •Emblems & nameplates

5. •Grille
6. •Header panel
7. •Hood inner panels
8. •Lamp aiming
9. •Mirror
10. •Moldings
11. •Mud guard
12. •Road wheel
13. •Spoilers & flares
14. •Stripe tape, decals, or overlays

Ask Yourself
If you are a new estimator, you need to get this list out and go over it for every part that you replace. Ask yourself if any of the non-included items are required to perform in the specific job that you are estimating. For instance, on the fender above ask: Will I have to R&I an antenna? If the fender has an antenna, add time for it on the estimate. If not, don't add it. Next, ask yourself if you will need to R&I bumper to replace the fender. If you will, add the time. If not, don't add any time for it. Go through each item on the non-included list and ask if this task will be required.

Increase Shop Profits
Now you can see the amount of money that you may leave unclaimed on each panel. Many of the non-included items will need to be performed on each fender you replace. Of course, you would only add what applies. You would not want to add time to R&I hood, if you do not need to remove the hood to R&R the fender. Look over the list on each panel that you estimate and add what applies

to the estimate. If a fender pays 3.0 hours, you may be able to add an extra .5 to 1.5 or more hours of non-included operations. This will lead to major profit for the company and technician at the end of a day. Who knows how much .2 or .3 for every emblem you replace may add up to at the end of one year.

Tell A Story
The key is to list each item separately. You need to tell a story with your estimate and it needs to be easy to understand. If you try to bulk or clump items together, chances are the insurance adjuster may refuse to pay.

Part 4 - The Labor Times Are Not Concrete

What Is Included In The Estimated Time
First of all, we call the estimating guide a guide for a reason. The labor times are not necessarily set in stone. If you feel the labor time or other issue is not fair you can challenge the task. There is a website for submitting your inquiries at http://degweb.org/ You may also want to check out this article on ABRN. Many times technicians and/or estimators do not feel like the estimating guide or computerized system gives enough time to perform the operation, but they just take it as the gospel as they do not know how to challenge the concern.

The Problem Will Only Be Corrected If They Know About It

If you truly feel that the guide is not giving you enough labor time, go to the above website and submit your concern, as there have been a lot of changes made to the different estimating guides due to this. The estimating software companies will never know that there is a problem with their database if we do not let them know.

How Are The Times Determined?

Let's discuss how the times are determined. The time is supposed to be the time it takes a skilled technician to perform the task. However, this is for new, undamaged parts. This does not include pulling damage to gain access to bolts, rusted or corroded bolts that may be harder to remove than new ones would. If this is necessary, you need to add the additional time to the estimate.

If The Guide Gives 3.0 Hours To R&R, What Is Included?

Let's discuss the fender that we said it would take 3.0 hours to R&R in an earlier section. This means that you are charging the customer 3.0 hours to take the old fender off and to put a new fender on the car.

Labor Rate

The shop labor rate is what the shop charges per hour. This varies depending on the shop as each shop is responsible for setting its own rate. In fact, it is against the law for shops to get together and discuss labor rates. That would be called price fixing. For this example, if the shop labor rate is $45, the shop would charge $135 to replace the fender. We will talk about paint and material charges later.

Estimating Times

All estimating guides use tenths. You may see 2.3, which is 2 hours and 18 minutes. There are 6 tenths in an hour so multiply each tenth by 6 to determine the time in minutes. .5 equals 30 minutes and 1.5 equals 1 hour and 30 minutes. This gives us an idea of how the labor times are determined.

Back To The Basics

We don't need to worry if the estimating system is correct or not at this time, as we're just getting started. I just wanted to give you an idea of how it works and that the times in the guides are not set in stone.

Part 5 - The Necessary Information
What Needs To Be On An Auto Estimate?

There are many different styles of estimate forms, but they all help you record the necessary information. All auto repair estimates will need to have your company information on it. It should also specify who the auto body estimator is and the estimator's contact information. It will need all of the customer's information, including their name, address, phone numbers, or any other contact information. I even like to get their e-mail address. The more contact information that you receive from the customer up front, the easier it will be to follow up or update the customer at a later time.

One Thing To Avoid
The last thing you want is to be hung up needing to speak to the owner before you can continue the repairs, only to discover that you cannot get in touch with him. Perhaps he goes on vacation and the only contact information that estimator recorded was his home phone number. You will not have a happy customer when he returns expecting his vehicle to be ready.

Vehicle Information
You will also need the vehicle information. The make, model, and style. Be certain to record the VIN number. This may be used to determine the correct parts to order and many other uses. The VIN can actually tell you quite a lot about the vehicle. Record the mileage, license plate number and the date. This is all important information to have for future purposes.

Insurance Information
Most accidents are going to be an insurance claim so be sure to get all of the insurance information. Insurance name, contact information, loss date, and type of loss.

Now You're Ready To Start Analyzing The Damage

Now you can get to the damage. Remember to follow the sequence of the estimating guide. If the accident is in the front, work from the front towards the back.

Get Information About The Accident

Before you start writing the damage, find out as much information as you can about the accident from the customer. The customer or whoever was in the accident is the best resource to get the information that you need to write a good estimate. A few of the questions that you may ask include: how many passengers were in the vehicle? You may need to examine the seat belt where a passenger was sitting. How fast were you traveling? Or, was the vehicle parked? What direction was each vehicle traveling upon impact? All of this information will help you have a better understanding of the accident and will help you write a better estimate.

A Communication Tool

Think of the estimate as a communication tool that will show the big picture. The more information you have on it, the clearer the big picture will look. The more customer, vehicle, insurance, and facts about the accident you collect, the better communications you will have throughout the entire process. A little extra work on the front side will save you a lot of time and headaches.

Part 6 - The Significance of Doing Your Best To Generate Auto Estimates

Once you have all of the information you need about the accident, you may choose to assist the customer and help them with a rental car or offer to give them a ride back to work or to their home. It may not be necessary for the customer to be there while you write the estimate. This is where many shops are rethinking the way they write estimates, rather than have the customer waiting and the estimator rushing through the estimating process so the customer does not have to wait long. Now many shops are assisting the customer with a rental car or a ride. This allows the estimator to write a thorough estimate, which may require disassembly of parts and/or raising the car off the ground to determine extent of damage. For example, the estimator or a technician may need to remove the front bumper to determine what parts are damaged behind the bumper cover. By inspecting the damage this way, you should have a very thorough estimate when completed. Before putting the car back together you may want to contact the customer (if you did not already have the customer authorize repairs) and discuss the repairs needed with them and the steps necessary to have the car repaired. If an insurance company is involved, you will also want to discuss repairs with them as well. This will let the insurance know that the customer has already authorized your shop to perform the repairs. If the insurance company demands that the car be taken to another shop, simply ask for the time spent tearing the car down and putting it back together. Chances are they will leave the car at your shop.

This is getting a little technical for now, but I just wanted to give you an idea of how it may work in the industry. There is currently a fight going on with the shops, as some insurance companies are trying to determine where the car will be repaired. However, that is called steering and it is illegal. But that does not seem to stop the insurance companies from doing it. This is definitely for another discussion or lesson.

The main point of this post is to write a thorough estimate as it serves many purposes. With today's complex cars, the days of writing a visual estimate without tear down are gone. Cycle times and the lean process are moving away from unnecessary work, which includes writing supplements on every vehicle that you work on. A well-written estimate will also give your technicians a better idea of what all they need to do to the vehicle. The estimate serves many purposes, but a communication tool should be a vital purpose. A communication tool between the shop, customer, insurance company, and the technician. Now you see the importance of the estimate. Therefore, you should try your absolute best on every single estimate that you generate.

Part 7 - Computerized Auto Estimates

Do you remember when businesses started implementing more computers? I kept hearing of how much paperwork this was going to save and how much easier the computers will make our work. Well, years later I'm still not fully convinced of that theory. It seems like we have more forms, files, and paperwork than we ever had before. I keep hearing paperless, but I am not seeing it. I think perhaps every item that goes paperless, there are two or three additional things that come up that we must manage. However, I do like the ways computers work and believe that we keep better records of everything. I think that we did not have a lot of the work because we were just not doing it. We really have all of our records at our fingertips even though it seems like a lot of work to manage.

It was painful getting to this point as an estimator. I remember the first computerized estimating system that Mitchell came out with. We had twice the amount of estimating guides to pack around and we still had to flip through the pages to swipe the bar codes. I did not like that system, but the systems that they have today make it much easier to write *auto repair estimates*. I mean, who can't point and click?

One of the advantages of computerized *auto repair estimates* is that there are no errors. Well, an auto estimator can still leave a lot of money on the table by not adding non-included operations, but computers have eliminated all of the calculation errors. It is pretty hard to misplace an estimate when it is stored in your computer as well.

Therefore, computers are more accurate and remove much of the human error out of the equation.

Most computer estimating systems update their information on a monthly basis. As fast as the parts prices can change, this is a big benefit as well. When we used the estimating guides, they were sent out every three months, which would be outdated before you received your new copy. The computer also eliminates a lot of writing. Remember how I said to list each item separately in an earlier post? Now you may only have to type a few of the operations that are not in the system. However, you can point and click most of your estimate with ease.

The internet also made it possible to work directly with insurance companies. Both the shop and the insurance can look at the same estimate online. They can also view digital photos. This was the birth of Direct Repair Program (DRP). This started out as a good thing, which allowed shops to partner with insurance claims handling processes, but the program took a different direction in my opinion. Insurance companies started demanding discounts and requiring the customers to use the shops that they had relationships with. Again, that is another subject that we may discuss at a later time. The internet and computers along with digital cameras have simplified the claims process.

Part 8 - What About Time Not In The Estimating Guide?

What about labor time not in the estimating guide or estimating system?

Not every operation is going to be included in the estimating guide. For instance, the labor time for all of the dent repair, plastic repair, frame repair, and many of the non-included operations in the p-pages are not in the guide. This is where experience steps in. When you have to determine the time it should take to repair a dent on a right front fender is called a judgment time because you are the judge and make the call. Therefore, judgment times can vary greatly from shop to shop or estimator to estimator.

Different Labor Rates

We already discussed that shops are responsible to set their own labor rates in an earlier section. Although, most shops charge different rates for the different types of operations they perform. For example, a shop may charge $45 for body labor, $45 for paint labor, $65 for frame and structural repair labor, and $75 for mechanical labor. As an estimator it is important to determine what each operation is to assure that it is labeled correctly. Many estimating guides have a "m" for mechanical operations and a "s" for structural operations. However, you must make sure that it is added into the correct category or you may not charge the different amounts. Therefore, if you are charging $45 for every operation, your shop and technicians are not making as much money as they should be making. Small details like this can add to a lot of additional income over a week or month time period.

Part 9 - Vehicle Information

Make and Model

Record the make and model of the vehicle. Is it a coupe, sedan, etc.? You will also want to record any packages that the vehicle is equipped with.

Decoding the VIN

The VIN stands for the Vehicle Identification Number. This number tells a lot about the vehicle. There are 17 characters in a VIN and each character tells something about the vehicle. This will vary depending on the manufacturer, but the first digit will let us know what country the vehicle was made in. The 10th digit will always let us know the year model. To determine what all of the characters stand for, you can look in the p-pages. This will help us decode the vehicle. If you're using a computer system, it will probably decode the VIN for us. In CCC Pathways you must put in the VIN to complete the estimate. Once the VIN is put into the computer correctly, CCC will decode the VIN for us. If you recorded the VIN wrong, you will not be able to proceed. So it is important to record it correctly. Writing it down correctly will also save you another trip to the car. Visit your p-pages to help you de-vin the VIN. A correct VIN will also help you when ordering parts to assure you are ordering the correct parts. Miss-ordered parts is an ongoing issue, which delays repairs, increases recycle times, and may break a promise date of completion to the customer.

Why Record Mileage?

Recording the mileage is easy to overlook when writing an estimate. However, it is important to get the mileage for several different reasons. The reason that I always like to record the mileage is for documentation. I have heard of customers claiming that their vehicle was driven around town using all of their gas. It may be necessary to test drive a vehicle before returning it to the customer, but the mileage recorded before repairs were made will give you documentation of actual miles the car was driven while in the shop for repairs. Always document everything, as it may cover your tail at a later time.

Date of Estimate

You will also need to record the date the vehicle was estimated. Normally an estimate is only good for one month. With price changes, the estimate may become invalid with incorrect prices, which will need to be adjusted. Another reason it is important to record the date the estimate was written is because the condition of the vehicle can change. For example, when you wrote the estimate, the vehicle may have had surface rust. Several months later the rust may turn into a panel that needs to be replaced or additional labor to repair the damage.

Prior Damage

Prior damage is damage that was present before the accident occurred. This is important to discover as insurance will not pay for prior damage. Prior damage may be on adjacent panels or it may be on the damaged panel that you are estimating. For example, if a vehicle has a small dent on the front of the right front fender with prior damage on the back of the right front fender, the insurance will not pay for the repair time for the damage to the rear of the fender. The damage will probably need to be repaired, but it will be at the cost of the customer, not the insurance companies.

Finding The Paint Code

Paint codes can be in various locations depending on make and model. The p-pages or your estimating system will usually give you the location of the paint code. You will need to know if the car has clear coat, tri-coats, or quad coats. This will all change the cost of paint labor and paint material costs, which we will talk about later.

Part 10 - The Different Types of Damage

I have briefly mentioned the different types of damage in previous parts. However, I would like to take some time to thoroughly discuss the different types of damage to look for when writing an *auto repair estimate.*

The most obvious damage is going to be direct damage. This is the point of impact, which is very easy to identify. When repairing a vehicle, we have the first in, last out rule. The point of impact would be the "first in" location of the damage. Therefore, this should be the last area to be repaired. The reason you need to know this as an estimator, is because if there is direct damage, there may also be indirect damage. This is the secondary damage, which is harder to identify. These are the damages that are caused by energy transfer during the collision. This may include buckles, popped spot welds, cracked seam sealer, and misaligned panel gaps. On unibody vehicles, secondary damage can occur throughout the entire vehicle, which will require a thorough inspection. There are actually five different damage zones during an accident.

1. •**Zone 1** is the direct damage as mentioned above, the point of impact.

2. •**Zone 2** is the indirect or secondary damage, which is caused from the force and direct damage.

3. •**Zone 3** is the mechanical component damage. I am sure that you've heard the law "an object in motion tends to stay on motion," well, your mechanical components like your engine, transmission, drive train, can cause damage when in an accident. If the engine is traveling at 50 mph and the vehicle comes to a sudden stop, the weight of the engine is still wanting to travel at 50 mph. This can cause damage to motor mounts and other attachment points.

4. •**Zone 4** is the passenger compartment. The same Newton law applies to people in the vehicle too. Passenger can cause damage to seat belts, knee bolster panels, and other interior parts. This may

also result in airbag deployment, which requires additional operations to repair the vehicle.

5.   • **Zone 5** includes exterior components and trim. These are items that are attached to the vehicle. These are additional items that can be damaged or create damage during an accident. Another thing you may consider when inspecting the vehicle for damage are items in the vehicle. Were there heavy items in the trunk space or in the passenger compartment? A flying tool box can create damage to the vehicle. These are some things to keep in mind when writing auto repair estimates. Go through each zone in your head looking for damage to the vehicle.

Next we'll discuss the predictable reaction a driver may have during an accident, so check back soon.

Part 11 - Accident Sequence

There are no absolutes when it comes to auto accidents. Although, there are some predicted actions that a driver usually makes during an accident. If you are traveling down the road and you see a car coming towards you, what are you going to do? Chances are that you will hit your brakes and/or turn away from the oncoming car or object. That is what most people's natural response is without thinking about it. If we consider that first action is hitting the brakes, it can help us determine what damage may be present. As you slam on the brakes you transfer the momentum of your car to the front as it goes down. While the front goes down the rear raises higher. When the impact happens it is safe to assume that the damage will be higher than if the brakes were not applied, which may cause more damage to transfer through the upper part of the vehicle and cause sag damage to the vehicle. However, many people have another response as well. You are normally going to turn your wheel away from the oncoming vehicle. As you do that, your car is now at an angle with the front end down and the rear high when the impact occurs. Now it is safe to assume that the vehicle may have side sway damage as well. If you keep this sequence of reactions in mind as you begin inspecting the vehicle with the 5 zones as mentioned in the previous part, you will begin to have a clear idea of what damage may be present and what to look for. This will help you generate a more thorough *auto repair estimate*.

Part 12 - Generating The Estimate
Begin the inspection

Now that you know what types of damage there may be and the sequence of predicted damage that may be present, we can begin to write the auto repair estimate. We have all of the customer information, vehicle information, and insurance information recorded on the estimate form. We have asked the driver of the vehicle all of the questions to determine what happened during the accident and any additional information that you may need. Now it is time to start writing the auto repair estimate. First you want to inspect the vehicle looking for all direct and secondary damage.

This may include:

Raising the vehicle up to look underneath the vehicle.

1. •

Looking inside the passenger compartment, measuring to determine if any frame or unibody damage is present, to determine the severity of the damage.

2. •

Visually inspecting all body gaps for misalignments, popped loose spot welds, cracked seam sealer, etc.

Once you have the big picture you can start writing the damage estimate report. Start with the damage that is near the front of the vehicle first and move backwards. For example, if the door, rocker panel, and rear quarter panel are damaged, write in that sequence. Most estimating guides and computer estimating systems follow the same sequence, front to back. Record everything that needs to be repaired or replaced on the estimate. This may require removing parts to determine if there is damage to the parts that we cannot see. Open all doors, hoods, and the deck lid. However, if the customer is going to be driving the vehicle after your inspection, you may not want to pry or wedge any parts open to gain access. This may lead to a panel that will not shut properly, which may be a safety hazard. Be sure to explain to the customer your concerns and let them know there will probably be hidden damage upon tear down, which will require a supplement estimate to be generated. As we mentioned in an earlier section, you may consider helping arrange rental or providing a ride for the customer once you have all of the necessary information from them. If you get the customer to go ahead and sign authorization for repairs, you can take your time and thoroughly write a clean estimate, which may require partial tear down. Once you have an auto damage estimate generated, you can consult with the customer and insurance adjuster to determine the next step of action to take.

Part 13 - Deducting For Overlap

Paint times are given in the estimating guides as well. In the Mitchell estimating guides, the refinish labor time, R&I time, O/H time are usually right under the title of each part. The R&R time is usually listed with the part. All paint times are determined for painting one panel at a time. However, many times we paint more than one part at a time. For example, if a car was hit in the front it may damage the hood and both front fenders. Therefore, three parts would be painted at the same time. Would it take the same amount of time to do all three panels at the same time as opposed to pulling the car in and out of the booth three separate times? Of course it would save time. You would only mask once, mix paint once, spray the paint once, and clean your spray gun once. Therefore, we should deduct part of the time for each additional panel that we paint. The first major panel will not have any deduction for overlap. However, each additional adjacent panel, the estimator needs to deduct .4. If it is not an adjacent panel, the estimator will need to deduct .2. In the example above we have a hood and two fenders. Let's say the guide gives 3.0 for each panel. With no deductions you would total 9.0 refinish hours. That would not be correct and adjustment would need to be made. Let's figure this deducting refinish labor correctly. The first major panel is the hood, which give us 3.0 hours. The next adjacent panel is the fender, which gives us 3.0. Since this is an adjacent panel, we will deduct .4 giving us 2.6. The next adjacent panel is the other fender, which gives us 3.0. We will deduct .4 from that time as well giving us 2.6. Now your total paint time will be 3.0+2.6+2.6= 8.2. This is .8 less time that we will charge after deducting overlap. Remember that panels that are not adjacent to the panel you're painting will only have .2 deducted per panel.

Here is an example of how this works on an estimate.

	Body Labor	Paint
Repair Hood Panel	2.5	3.0
Deduct for paint overlap		.0
Adjusted Paint Time		**3.0**
Repair Right Front Fender	2.0	3.0
Deduct for paint overlap		-.4
Adjusted Paint Time		**2.6**

Repair Left Front Fender	1.0	3.0
Deduct for paint overlap		-.4
Adjusted Paint Time		**2.6**
Total Labor	**5.5**	**8.2**

Part 14 - Adding For Clear Coat

When writing auto repair estimates the auto estimator must add for clear coat. The clear coat takes time to spray onto the vehicle and it is expensive. Therefore, there should be a charge for the time that it takes to mix and apply it and a charge for a cost of the material. The time should be added to refinish labor to accomplish both labor time and material charge. We will discuss how to determine the material charge later in another section.

Today we are going to explain why you must add for clear coat and how to determine how much time to add. You may be thinking that most vehicles have clear coat; why doesn't the guide include the time it takes to clear? This is because not all cars have clear coat, and you should not get paid for an operation that you did not perform. I think it is fair for technicians to get paid for everything that they do, but if we start charging for things that we don't do, it's fraud and can lead to a lot of trouble. So if you're going to add for clear or any other non-included operations, make sure it needs it.

If you clear one panel, you will need to mix your clear, tack the surface that you're spraying, spray the clear on the panel, and clean your spray gun. To add for clear coat you add 40% of the time given to paint the panel. If you spraying a panel with 3.0 hours, you would multiply 3.0 x 40% = 1.2. So to paint and clear this panel you have 3.0+1.2 = 4.2 Total Paint Time.

For each additional panel you will need to deduct for overlap then add 20% for clear coat. For example, if the adjacent panel gives 3.0 hours we will deduct .4 to give us 2.6. Now multiply 2.6 x 20% = .5. Add 2.6 + clear time of .5 top get a total of 3.1 paint time to paint and clear the adjacent panel. This same formula will apply to each additional panel. Deduct overlap and multiply by 20%.

Let's take a look of the example in the previous post.

	Body Labor	Paint
Repair Hood Panel	2.5	3.0
Deduct for paint overlap		.0
Add For Clear Coat		1.2
Adjusted Paint Time w/ clear		**4.2**
Repair Right Front Fender	2.0	3.0
Deduct for paint overlap		-.4

Adjusted Paint Time		2.6
Add For Clear Coat		.5
Adjusted Paint Time w/ clear		**3.1**

Repair Left Front Fender	1.0	3.0
Deduct for paint overlap		-.4
Adjusted Paint Time		2.6
Add For Clear Coat		**.5**
Adjusted Paint Time w/ clear		**3.1**

Total Labor	**5.5**	**10.4**

Part 15 - Add For Tri-Coat

Adding for tri-coat or three stage paint is similar to adding for clear coat. However, you will need to know when to add for clear coat and when to add for tri-coat. Tri-coat consists of base coat, mid-coat and clear coat, which is three different operations that you must do to get the paint to match. The mid-coat may be a pearl coat or tinted clear to create different effects, including shifting colors and adding more depth. It may be very difficult to determine by looking if it is a tri-coat or not. To be certain if you are charging for the correct operation, locate the paint code on the vehicle and look it up. The paint code is NOT part of the VIN number. It is a code that is located in various places on a vehicle. The p-pages will give you some general ideas of where these paint code labels may be located and will help you identify tri-coat colors.

When adding for tri-coat you do not add for clear coat. The clear coat time is included in the tri-coat application. Use the same formula by deducting for overlap and for adding clear, except add 70% per refinish hour to your first panel and 40% to each additional panel.

Let's examine the same example that we've been discussing with tri-coat.

	Body Labor	Paint
Repair Hood Panel	2.5	3.0
Deduct for paint overlap		.0
Add For Tri-Coat		2.1
Adjusted Paint Time w/ tri-coat		**5.1**
Repair Right Front Fender	2.0	3.0
Deduct for paint overlap		-.4
Adjusted Paint Time		2.6
Add For Tri-Coat		1.0
Adjusted Paint Time w/ tri-c		**3.6**
Repair Left Front Fender	1.0	3.0
Deduct for paint overlap		-.4
Adjusted Paint Time		2.6
Add For Tri-Coat		1.0
Adjusted Paint Time w/ tri-c		**3.6**
Total Labor	**5.5**	**12.3**

Part 16 - Adding For Two-Tone

Two-tones are not included in the time given to refinish a panel. Two-tone means there are two different colors on the vehicle. Again, we use a simple formula to determine the time to estimate for this operation. Before we discuss two-tones I am going to touch on edging and painting the undersides of panels. In all of the examples that we have had, we only repaired the parts. Normally when you repair a part, the jamb or inside of the panel does not need to be repainted. However, any time you replace the part it will be necessary to paint the inside. For example, if we replace a right front fender and it pays 3.0, that does not include the inside. All you need to do is look in the estimating guide and it will give you the time for edging or to paint the inside of the panel. The right front fender may state to add .5 for edging. This would give you a total paint time of 3.5 to paint the right front fender.

Now back to two-tone. The reason that I mention edging now is this. Many new cars have different color schemes for the insides of the panels. Therefore, you should be able to add for two-tone. I don't know if shops are adding two-tone for this operation, but it may be something to consider. To add for two-tone, add 50% per refinish hour for your first major panel and 30% for each additional panel. Basically, it is the same formula as clear coat, just different numbers to plug in. However, this does not add the clear coat as tri-coat does. It is possible to have a single stage two-tone so clear it is not figured into the two-tone time.

If the first panel gives 3.0 to refinish the panel, you would multiply 3.0 x 50% = 1.5. Then you would add for clear coat by multiplying 3.0 x 40% = 1.2. This would give you a total of 5.7 hours to paint, two-tone and clear coat the panel.

Let's take a look at the same example that we've been working on and determine what the refinish time will be with two-tone added.

	Body Labor	Paint
Repair Hood Panel	2.5	3.0
Deduct for paint overlap		.0
Add For Two-Tone		1.5
Add For Clear		1.2
Adjusted Paint Time		**5.7**
Repair Right Front Fender	2.0	3.0
Deduct for paint overlap		-.4
Adjusted Paint Time		2.6
Add For Two-Tone		.8
Add For Clear		.5
Adjusted Paint Time		**3.9**
Repair Left Front Fender	1.0	3.0
Deduct for paint overlap		-.4
Adjusted Paint Time		2.6

Add For Two-Tone		.8
Add For Clear		.5
Adjusted Paint Time w/ tri-c		**3.9**
Total Labor	**5.5**	**13.5**

Part 17 - What To Charge For Materials

Itemizing Materials

This is an evolving process as we determine what we should charge for. There are systems available today that we did not have when I used to write estimates. Systems like PMC Logic will help you itemize the materials actually used on a repair. This makes it easy for the insurance adjuster and/or customer to see exactly what all materials were needed to repair the vehicle. However, if you do not use a system like this, you must be certain to write everything that you use on the estimate. If we state exactly what we use and charge for it, chances are that insurance company will pay for it. Remember, they need to CYA too. If they can show their supervisor why they paid a certain amount for materials, this will make it easier for them as well. In fact, I have had several adjusters tell me that if the materials are itemized on the invoice, they will pay it. However, lump summing everything together in one line called materials needed, will not go far when the insurance company sees the invoice. Just like my Wal-Mart story. To determine if you were overcharged or not, you need to see exactly what you were charged for. Once you see that everything looks right, you feel better about paying that amount. However, if Wal-Mart gave us a receipt in one lump sum, we would probably think that they were wrong.

Traditional
The way materials have traditionally been charged for is from your refinish labor. You take the total amount of refinish labor hours and multiply it by a determined number. We used to multiply it by 50% of the refinish labor, but with the increase in materials costs, the number is usually higher now. For example, if the refinish labor is $40 per hour, the charge for materials will be $20 or higher for materials. So if you charged 3.0 hours to paint a fender and materials charge rate is $20.00, then the material charge will be $60 for paint materials.

What Is Not Calculated
What this method does not pay for is any adhesives, fillers, clips, etc. that you may use. With the price of these materials, you can lose money if you're not careful. Therefore, be certain to add the materials that are not included in the refinish labor time. Another thing that can cost you is not charging for all of your refinish time. For example, if no time is given to refinish a frame rail, you lose refinish time and material charges. If you overlook a half hour of labor (.5) this will cost you 20 dollars labor and 10 dollars materials for a total of 30 dollars. If you overlook something small like that 4 times a week that is $120 loss to the shop that week. If it happens more than that, then I think you can see how this could cut profits.

Charging For Materials From The Refinish Time

Let's take a look at the same example that we've been working on and determine what the material charges will be. We're going to use $40 for the labor rate and $20 for the material rate.

	Body	Paint	Lab
Repair Hood Panel	2.5		3.0
Deduct for paint overlap			.0
Add For Two-Tone			1.5
Add For Clear			1.2
Adjusted Paint Time			**5.7**
Repair Right Front Fender	2.0		3.0
Deduct for paint overlap			-.4
Adjusted Paint Time			2.6
Add For Two-Tone			.8
Add For Clear			.5
Adjusted Paint Time			**3.9**
Repair Left Front Fender	1.0		3.0
Deduct for paint overlap			-.4
Adjusted Paint Time			**2.6**
Add For Two-Tone			.8
Add For Clear			.5

Adjusted Paint Time w/ tri-c		**3.9**
Total Labor	**5.5**	**13.5**

13.5 is the refinish time

13.5 x 20 = 270 (if the material charge is 20)

So the material charge for this job would be $270.00

There is a lot more to estimating, but this will give you a basic understanding of how the estimating process works.

Parts & Accessory Resources
You Will Need To Access This From The E-Book Format or the Members Website To Access The Links.

4 Wheel Parts - Parts & Accessories

Auto Accessories Garage - Covers, Bras, Seats, etc.

Advantage Auto Parts - Auto Parts

Andy's Auto Sport - Carbon Fiber - Lambo Doors, Etc.

Auto Barn - Auto Parts and Accessories

Auto Parts Giant - Parts & Accessories

Auto Parts Supplies - Auto Parts

Auto Parts Warehouse - Parts Finder

carID - Auto Parts and Accessories

Car-Parts - Used Parts

Phantom Alert - Radar, GPS, Red Light Detector

Genesis Auto Parts - Radiators, Condensers, fuel pumps, etc.

Goodmark - Restoration Parts

JC Whitney - Parts & Acc. Note: sheet metal body parts are not (CAPA) parts.

Junk Car - Sell Your Junk Car

KeyStone Automotive - (CAPA) Recommended For Aftermarket (sheet metal) Parts

LMC Truck - Pick-up Truck Parts

Motorcycle Super Store - Motorcycle Parts

National Trailer Supply - Trailer Supplies

Proper Auto Care - Car Care Products
Salvage Auctions
Sheet Metal Direct
Street Side Automotive - Performance Auto Parts
The Clip House - Auto Clips, Weatherstripping,
Restoration
Tire Rack - Tires
Vivid Racing - Racing Parts and Accessories
YearOne - Restoration Parts

Supplies

3M - Body Shop Supplies
Autobody Tool Mart
C&H Supplies - Industrial Storage Supplies
Meguires - Detailing Supplies
Proper Auto Care - Detailing Supplies
TPC Global - Body Shop and Paint Supplies

Tool

Harbor Freights - Low Quality, But Cheap Tools
Mac Tools
TBC Global - Paint Guns
Snap-on Tools
Sears - Tools

Other

Angies List - Local Business Reviews
AutoCheck - Vehicle History Report

ClaimBuster - How To Deal With Adjusters and Attorneys
Craigslist - Free Local Classified
Enterprise Car Rental
Fox Car Rental
Lease Trader - Car Leases

Small Business Ideas/ Add Ons

Bumper Doc - PDR, Paint Touch-Up Ect. Franchise
CARSTAR - Body Shop Business Franchise
Collision On Wheels - Mobile Collision Repair Franchise - Not sure how they stay compliant!
Dash Topper - Become A Dash Topper Dealer
Ding King - Paintless Dent Repair Franchise
Rhino Liners - Sprayed On Bed Liner Dealer
Touch Up Guys - Car Appearance Franchise
Windshield Repair - How To
Xtreme Liners - Sprayed On Bed Liner Dealer
Brake Basics
How To Change Your Oil
How To Keep Battery Fully Charged
How To Replace Shocks
How To Replace Rear Hatch Strut Supports - For lift hatch doors that will not stay up.

Student Resources

You Will Need To Access This From The E-Book Format or the Members Website To Access The Links.

2. NATEF Schools
3. Scholarships
4. Study Skills Guide
5. What is an Resume
6. HowTo Resume
7. Example Resume
8. Letter of Recommendation
9. Jobs
10. Job Interviews
11. Starting A Business
12. Buy or Rent Textbooks - Online Textbooks
13. MySpace
14. FaceBook
15. Franklin Covey
16. Linked In
17. YouTube
18. Edmunds - Car website
19. Hub Garage - Social Network for car enthusiast
20. Couch Surfing - A network for college students to travel for free.
21. ChaCha - Online search with live answers.
22. Online Textbooks
23. Office and School Supplies
24. Rent Textbooks
25. Snopes - Rumor or fact? Find the truth behind the story.
26. Dictionary/Encyclopedia

27. <u>Discovery Channel</u>
28. <u>World Book Store</u>
29. <u>CampusGrotto</u> - Known as the "inside source" for college students, CampusGrotto is a national College News site that focuses on college life. Some of the topics covered include: student finances, college scholarships, career advice and studying.
30. <u>CollegeTips</u> - Featuring real tips from college students, CollegeTips.com provides advice that can't be found in college packets. New articles are added every week.
31. <u>Gearfire</u> - This website provides tips for academic success. Gearfire contributors range from high school students to college graduates.
32. <u>CollegeBoard</u> - The CollegeBoard website has a staggering amount of quality information for college students. Most of the info is meant for students applying to college, but a few articles are directed at current students as well.
33. <u>College@Home</u> - This hidden gem is a fine place to find school reviews and open courseware. College@Home also has a fantastic blog with tons of lists like: <u>50 Ways to Greenify Your Campus</u> and <u>57 Time Management Hacks for College Students</u>.

Changing The Perception Of Auto Body 101

"Shop class," such as Auto Body or Automotive has had a reputation of changing its meaning through the years in the eyes of the public. It has gone through the transition of cool hot rods, racing, restoration, or hobby class to easy "A" for the slackers or even a holding place for students that the high school counselors don't know what else to do with. There are many reasons that contribute to the lack of qualified students entering technical education courses, but we may be in for a rude awakening if we don't pay attention and change our thinking. In order for us to protect ourselves from unskilled technicians, who will lead to unsafe vehicles on the road, our educational system must put the same emphasis on technical education (auto body, welding, etc.) as they do academic skills (math, English, etc.). Part of the reason schools are giving the technical programs less attention is due to bill that was passed by the Bush administration called "No Child Left Behind." Bush has constantly pushed to stop all funding to technical education programs, in order to increase funds to the NCLB act. With this action, the mentality is that all students can learn. Therefore, all students should attend a four-year school after graduating high school.

However, according to the National Assessment of Vocational Education (NAVE) "two-thirds of young people do not obtain a four-year degree and 25% of them go directly to work after high school" (NAVE 6). According to this study, our perception of all students attending a four-year degree is incorrect. What are we doing with the two-thirds of students not attending a four-year college? Shouldn't we focus more on these students?

The NCLB bill has forced schools to focus on academic skills, which improve students' math, English, etc. in order to secure their funding. Therefore, schools are using every student who is competent of performing well academically to comply with the (NCLB) standard for better test scores. This leaves less room for technical education, which does not directly prepare students for the state assessment tests. In some cases, programs such as Auto Body are receiving students that the school does not know what else to do with. Many of these students are at risk of dropping out of school, low performing, and low motivated.

With the quality students' shop classes are receiving in mind, let's discuss modern-day vehicles. Since there have been cars, there has been pride. Many people feel like their car is part of the family. If it's involved in an accident, they are concerned and want it repaired back to the perfect condition that it was in before the collision. If the vehicle was not returned back to the owner in its pre-accidental condition, they are crushed and their pride is destroyed. However, there is more than pride that will be crushed if modern day vehicles are not repaired back to their pre-accidental condition. Now, if a modern-day sophisticated vehicle is improperly repaired, it will result in unnecessary injuries or deaths to you or your whole family.

According to the US Federal Government National Highway Traffic Safety Administration, as stated on caraccidents.com in 2005 there were nearly 6,440,000 auto accidents with a financial cost of more than 230 billion dollars. More importantly, 2.9 million people were injured and 42,636 people were killed. That averages 115 people who die per day, which is one every 13 minutes.

How many of these wrecked vehicles are repaired and back on the road? Of those repaired, how many of them were repaired correctly? There are organizations, like I-CAR, available to educate technicians in the collision industry, but it takes a competent technician to be able to absorb and apply what he or she has learned. If he or she is unable to comprehend the content, this will jeopardize the repairs made to the vehicle, which could result in an unnecessary injury or death as mentioned above. Therefore, Auto Body 101 is more critical to society then you may have realized. It's crucial to focus on these types of programs to eliminate some of those injuries and deaths.

Why are improperly repaired vehicles a bigger threat now than they used to be? The reason is the fast-paced technology modern-day cars have. Our cars have all of these cool features that make our lives easier. However, relying on some of these features will create a death trap if they are not working properly.

If you visit the official Chevrolet Malibu website you will see that it comes equipped with OnStar, turn-by-turn navigation, hands-free calling, stabilitrak, and six air bags. This car sounds to be safe, and it is. It was named 2008 car of North America car of the year. It has 5 star frontal and side crash test rating. OnStar now allows the vehicle to give you turn-by-turn direction. The Malibu will even diagnose itself and e-mail the results to you. Another safety feature is the hands-free calling. I know I have came close to an accident due to answering a cell phone call or dialing a number while driving. The stabilitrak sends messages to the computer and automatically adjusts your suspension depending on the road conditions and will help prevent you from having an accident. These features are great; however, when involved in an accident, it can become complicated to assure everything is repaired correctly. In addition to the traditional body and paint work, we must focus on all of the safety and electrical work as well. I think we are already starting to understand that we need properly trained and highly skilled automotive and collision repair technicians to work on our vehicles.

In addition to airbags, car makers are looking at other ways to increase safety as John Quain writes in the New York Times. Everyone knows airbags provide safety, but car makers are starting to look at other issues. John writes that over 100 children are backed over and killed every year. To prevent this, the car makers are putting cameras in vehicles allowing the driver to see behind better. This is just a start of what we are seeing in modern-day vehicles. However, the features that keep us safer are all vulnerable to damage during a collision. The technician must be much more knowledgeable about electronics to properly repair a vehicle back to its pre-accidental condition.

If you pick up an auto body textbook by James Duffy, you will learn about vehicle construction. The first frames, ladder frames, were designed to hold a car body on the top of it. However, the frame did not provide safety when involved in an accident. Imagine for a minute that you are strapped down to a heavy duty extension ladder. Now imaging that you hit a brick wall traveling at 50 mph. When you hit the wall you will come to a sudden stop and the impact would be deadly. Now imaging taking the extension ladder and placing some weaker points to the front of the ladder, which will collapse if involved in an accident. While these point collapse, it slows the ladder down before the sudden stop. This would cushion your collision. That is what car designers have done through the years to improve safety. The points that collapse are called crush zones. This can be indentions in the metal, which allow the frame and body panels to crush or collapse in a predictable manner.

At the same time, car designers are making the passenger compartment stronger to prevent the impact from injuring the passengers. This is done with different types of metals and materials. Some of the materials used in car structures and panels include: mild steel, high strength steel, ultra high strength steel, boron steel, aluminum, magnesium, sheet molded compound, plastic, and carbon fiber. Laser rolled steel allows the manufacturer to provide parts with different thicknesses. For example, a pillar may be thicker in certain areas and thinner in other areas. With this technology, the crush zones may not even be visible. This is significant because if a technician does not know where the crush zones are, it may result in an improper section procedure. For example, let's imagine a hood panel. We know that if you are involved in a front-end collision, the hood is going to buckle up. However, let's say that the hood had some additional supports welded underneath to strengthen it. If this vehicle is now involved in a front-end collision the additional braces will prevent the hood from buckling. This would result in the hood coming through the windshield, which may result in a death. A hood is one example, but the whole vehicle is designed with crush zones throughout the vehicle. If the technician can't see the crush zone, he or she may not know that a repair should not be performed in that area. He or she must be able to find the proper repair procedures. The traditional methods will not work for modern-day vehicles. This will require excellent reading and comprehension skills to locate and perform the needed repair procedure.

Earlier we discussed the high-tech technology an average priced car has today. Now let's look at one of the features of a higher priced car like BMW. On their official website you can learn about the car's steering capabilities. The car's steering range changes depending on the speed you're going. For instance, at slow speed you don't have to turn the steering wheel much to make sharp turns. At higher speed it takes more movement of the steering wheel to make turns. This is a really cool feature, but the steering components are bolted directly to today's unibody structures. Therefore, if the car is involved in an accident, the structure is vulnerable to damage. In the past, technicians could pull the structure back to its correct dimensions, give or take a little. Then the front end could be aligned to assure the car will drive properly. However, today's cars allow very little tolerance. The structure must be pulled almost exactly back to its factory dimensions. If not, the front end may never align properly, as there are not any adjustments to adjust on newer vehicles. There is not much adjustment on body panels today either. If the structure is slightly off, this will result in door, hood, and fender gaps misaligned. This requires a technician to be accurate, skilled, and the ability to use mathematical skills.

The consumer is not the only one at risk; an incompetent technician is at risk as well. In an article by I-CAR, the topic of multiple-stage airbags is discussed. Depending on the impact, one or two bursts may inflate the airbag. In a light impact the first stage may only fire. This allows the airbag to be inflated long enough to protect the passenger. However, in a hard impact, the impact force is greater and takes longer before completely stopped. Therefore the second charge fires immediately after the first charge to keep the air bag inflated longer for added protection. The added protection is great for the safety protection to the passengers; however, it can be deadly to the untrained technician. If a technician physically sees that the air bag has deployed, this may have him or her believe that there is no risk of accidentally deploying it. However, if it is a two-stage system, it could deploy again during repairs, which could result in injury or death to the technician. It's little things like this that may take the untrained technician out of this business permanently.

Another example is the magnesium used in some vehicle parts today. If an unskilled technician determines that he or she needs to make a weld repair on or too close to a radiator support, this could result in severe burns to them, as the radiator support of newer model Ford pick-ups are made out of magnesium. There have been reports of vehicles being burned to the ground in body shops for this reason. If a technician can read and comprehend proper repair procedures, he should not have any problems with safety. However, steering students who are unmotivated and will not perform well in any of their classes to this profession is putting them at risk. We need highly motivated students with academic and technical skills to enter this career pathway.

I think we have conveyed the significance of the safety issues of repairing vehicles back to their pre-accidental condition. Now let's look at what the American Society for Training and Development (ASTD) says about required competencies in the book titled Overview of Career and Technical Education by John Scott. Following are the seven skill groups compromising the workplace basics identified in the ASTD report: Foundational-Learning to Learn, Competence-Reading, Writing, and Computation, Communication-Listening and Oral Communications, Adaptability-Creative Thinking and Problem Solving, Personal Management-Self Esteem, Goal Setting/Motivation, and personal/Career Career Development, Group Effectiveness-Interpersonal Skills, Negotiating, and Teamwork, Influence-Organizational Effectiveness and Leadership (Scott 9-10). This sums up the fact that technical careers need highly qualified students entering these professions. For example, a collision repair technician must be able to communicate well with the managers and customers. Miscommunication is one of the biggest problems business managers face. A technician must be able to read the repair order to determine what repairs are needed to the vehicle and what may not be included in the repair process.

The technician will also need good reading and comprehension skills to locate and determine the manufacture repair procedures. Mathematical skills are essential to properly measure a damaged frame or unibody structure. It also takes mathematical skills to measure paints and ensure proper mixing ratios. However, if you talk to body shop managers, one of the common things they are looking for is good work ethics and a good attitude. As you can see, it takes a rounded set of technical, academic, and professional skills to succeed in technical careers.

Allowing students to explore career opportunities to find their interests and talents is an important role for education to play. In fact, there are many students who are bored in academic classes. Some of these students are gifted and intelligent; however, they lose interest and sight and find themselves dropping out of high school. California Governor Schwarzenegger is a big advocate of technical education and discusses it as being a solution to keeping students in school. In an article in Time Magazine he states, "I have talked to many kids who tell me they don't want to go to college, so why graduate? They don't see an end goal. They can't visualize it." The governor strives to attain additional funding for vocational programs in California. He understands the value and role it plays in society. While technical careers may not be for everyone, I believe education needs to do a better job of promoting and allowing students to explore all career opportunities allowing them to find their niche.

Would you rather go to an incompetent heart or brain surgeon or an incompetent collision repair technician? You may be quick to say an incompetent technician, but if you think about it for a little bit you may realize that the doctor could jeopardize your life. However, a collision repair technician could jeopardize your life, in addition to your family's life and others. As mentioned earlier, 115 people die every day in the U.S. due to auto accidents. I don't think that many people die going to the doctor. This puts it in a different perspective, doesn't it? We'd better keep the slackers out of the health industry and the collision repair industry. Our educational system needs to put the same emphasis on technical education as they do academic skills in order to assure we have properly trained technicians for our future. If we don't expose the different professions to students, then we will pay the consequences for it later.

ABOUT THE AUTHOR

My passion for working on cars started when I was a kid. I helped my dad and older brother work on cars as a hobby.

In high school I enrolled in auto shop and painted my first car. After stepping back and seeing the finished product, I knew that I was hooked for life. After graduating high school I attended the collision repair program at WyoTech. Since then I have worked for body shops and a body tech, paint tech, and an estimator. I have managed and owned a body shop. For the past 7 years I have been teaching collision repair for an NATEF Accredited school that is also a member of the I-CAR Industry Training Alliance. I stay up-to-date with the collision repair industry by attending training on a continuing basis, I am a member of ASA and the active in the collision repair industry with my website http://CollisionBlast.com If you are not already a member of our network, I encourage you to join us. There you will receive additional training, news and networking with other in the collision repair industry.

Here Are A Few Of My Qualifications:
*Graduated WyoTech in 1988 and Have Years Of Experience
* Associates Degree in Collision Repair and Management
* Obtaining a Degree in Professional Technical Education
* ASE Certified
* PPG Certified
* I-CAR Instructor Work Shop Certified
* Member of ASA
* Custom Paint Certificate From WyoTech
* Custom Metal Working Certificate from UTI
* Numerous Other Certificates in Collision Repair and Teaching
* Attend SEMA, NACE, VISION and Many Other Training Events
*Technical Educator

I am not bragging with all of my qualifications as I will be the first to admit that I do not know it all. I still learn every day in this fast-paced industry. However, I do qualify to teach and I may be able to help you out if you're interested in collision repair and painting.
I have offered my training videos free in the past and here is what motivated me to do that and to develop this online training course book at the very low cost.
(1) You're interested in collision repair as a career. If so, this will allow you to test the career pathway and determine if collision repair is a fit for you. If it is, I

encourage you to further your education by enrolling in a college or technical school that provides collision repair. If you need help locating a NATEF accredited school in your area let me know. I have a list of all schools accredited throughout the U.S.

(2) You're interested in this as a hobby (DIY). If so, I would like to give you a pat on the back and help you all that I can. Believe it or not, you play a crucial role in the industry.

Without the DIY folks out there, there would not be any interest in the auto industries. Remember I said that I started working on cars with my dad and older brother as a kid? Well, we were just DIY people, which resulted in a collision repair career for me. I think there are many similar stories out there. I sincerely believe that it would improve any parent-child relationship. Your kids may not remember all of the TV shows or video games play growing up, but they will remember the times spent together working on a hobby, such as working on cars. Therefore, I want to give you all of the resources you need to make that happen. In return, you are providing interest and exposure to the collision repair career. It's win/win for everyone!

As you may know, I also provide free training videos for collision repair. However, I did get many of the same complaints and requests. The complaints have been not being able to hear the videos. Well, we are not professional video makers, but I have it fixed.

More text and audio for you to review. Another complaint was not specifying exactly what products I was using and some even wanted the parts numbers. I've got that covered too. I have added many of the products numbers that I use and like in the book. No, I did not cover every brand, just some of the products that I am familiar with. If I listed every brand of body filler and paint, I'd never get done with this book.

Besides, it would just be confusing to you as well. And I have been asked many times to do a more in-depth training course. Again, I listened to you all and here it is. I believe you have more relevant resources at your fingertips that you will find at any other single place. With all of this work and research, I had to charge a little for it. Believe me, if money was not an issue, I'd just give it to you all for free.

In this book I have included how-to articles, videos, and resources to help you on your training journey. So buckle your seat belt, sharpen your pencil, and get ready to learn paint and body repair work. Also, if you have any questions, feel free to contact me. I will do my best to help you find the answer if I do not have it. Thanks again and enjoy the online e-book course.

I have included many of the product information resources, technical data sheets and the MSDS if I was able to locate them. Be certain to read the technical data sheets before attempting to use the products. They are full of useful information. The MSDS Material Safety Data Sheets will inform you of the hazardous and ingredients in the product.

One thing that I would like to clarify….don't sweat the small stuff. In other words, keep it simple. There are many "correct" ways to get from point A to point B in this industry. There are certainly things you must avoid, but go with the flow. You may hear a little variation from one training system to another. For example, I-CAR may suggest doing it this way, while 3M suggests doing something a little different. Just focus on the end result and what is going to get you there. The reason that I bring this up is because I have provided training from many different resources and there are small variations in techniques. But don't worry, I have visited the content and found it to be a reliable and a relevant source. If I add something that I am not sure about, I will let you know.

Enjoy the training!

Donnie Smith